Introduction to Cognietrics

On the Psychology of Philosophy

Alon Oscar Deutsch

ISBN-10: 1539927652
ISBN-13: 978-1539927655

DEDICATION

This book is dedicated to my family with love.

"…Socionics and spin-off Cognietrics provide leverage which could possibly be adapted toward the enhancement of information flow…" – Marc Carson, Livingry and Building Technological Leverage to Change the World

CONTENTS

ACKNOWLEDGMENTS

I would like to thank Vered Deutsch for editing this book during her vacation time, and I would like to thank Mikey Goldenberg for using his degree in philosophy to help me address some of the epistemological concepts in this book.

PREFACE

I wrote my first book, An Introduction to Cognietrics, in order to bring extended meaning to the suppositions encountered in the definition of the Myers-Briggs types. Though many books have been written on this subject, I felt that few had unifying ideas or were otherwise able to inspire a coherent, philosophical discussion of its implications among readers. In writing this book I was finally able to redefine and then derive the fundamental epistemological concepts on which our experience of reality is based using underlying cognitive constructs, ultimately merging psychology with philosophy itself, and even discuss ideas that I had not previously encountered, such as the definition of knowledge in terms of Jungian dichotomies, the mathematical symmetry of philosophy, the principles on which the paradoxical Copenhagen Interpretation of quantum mechanics is founded, and the differences between induction and deduction, patterns and concepts, discovery and invention, cause and effect, and statistics and determinism. These ideas appear repeatedly in the philosophical literature - for instance, an example of Cognietrics in epistemology is the following: on page 1 of Introduction to Mathematical Philosophy, Bertrand Russell states that 'The distinction between mathematics and mathematical philosophy is one which depends upon the interest inspiring the research, and upon the stage which the research has reached.' When one considers that due to attained importance, and given the change associated with stages, something reaches a stage not necessarily when one can begin to think differently about it but rather when he can begin to feel differently about it due to its own unchanging state, and that while research is inspired by logic interest is inspired by emotion, it is obvious that

Russell is (perhaps unknowingly) referring to the Cognietric distinction between knowledge and understanding as outlined in my book; note that in the preface to Our Knowledge of the External World, which predates Carl Jung's Psychological Types by 7 years, Russell tries to shed new light on the distinction between 'realists and idealists', not unlike the Jungian dichotomy of sensation vs. intuition. In this book I also show how the different personalities work together to accommodate novel ideas and recurring trends in an endless cycle as determined by the order of the strongest Jungian Cognitive Functions, and I describe how different combinations of personality traits may manifest in each type. I provide research supporting the existence of mutually exclusive personality traits in accordance with the Myers-Briggs dichotomies, and explanations for the Jungian Cognitive Functions that I use to create a short test to aid in analyzing one's Jungian type. I also discuss theories of type development over time, and I provide background on previous typology theories such as Myers-Briggs and Socionics. I answer frequently asked questions on the nature, relevance, and justification of Jungian typology, and I discuss the benefit of mindfulness with respect to both of the values representing each dichotomy. There may be more fitting pattern models or those for which cognitive controls have less value though often the new perspectives generated thusly are useful. I must end by saying that I sincerely hope that this book brings you as much insight while reading it as it brought me while writing it, and I wish you the best of luck.

Alon Oscar Deutsch

Boca Raton, Florida

Friday, November 4th, 2016

CHAPTER ONE

Introduction

INTP, ISFP, ENFJ - what does it all mean? This book will show you what to expect when you come across one of these abbreviations. Drawing on references to epistemology, mathematics, physics, and even competing measures of intelligence, this book will explain how each Jungian type engages life.

Related Topics: Psychology, Typology, Personality, Jung, Myers-Briggs, Socionics

Why write a book?

After studying Jungian personality theories for many years, I wanted to clarify some inconsistencies between them and tell the world what it is I really have come to believe. The main idea in this book is that the behaviors defining the Jungian personalities can be derived from a combination of unique philosophical rationales which exist behind each one. Cognietrics is not meant to be a complete "Lexicon of the Psyche", but it is also not vague, and makes specific predictions based on my own personal experiences and impressions of different people. I have tried to make Cognietrics the most accurate, precise, and revealing representation of the best ideas (including many of my own) commonly found in analogous personality models. I hope that this book will not only allow you to understand yourself, but also allow you to understand others, so that you may find common interests or at least learn from each other.

As for self-development, there are many that say that the point of personality theory is to identify Weaknesses to improve them on the path to self-actualization and becoming a well-rounded person, such that less conscious Functions become more developed later in life. There are some who say that if you know your Strengths you can work on them and achieve more than if you try to compensate Weaknesses, which aren't likely to improve to the point of being competitive with others having them as Strengths. I believe that any work that is done to improve the use of any Function is beneficial, but I believe that using a balanced combination of Weak and Strong Functions works best.

Background

The Myers-Briggs Type Indicator (MBTI) was developed during and after WWII by Isabel Briggs-Myers and her mother Katherine Cook-Briggs. It was based on the earlier work of Carl Gustav Jung and was intended to help distribute different jobs in an efficient manner according to each job's suitability for a given psychological Preference.

Completion of the MBTI results in one of sixteen Types, each with a unique four-letter designation, with each letter representing a Preference.

The first letter can be E (Extraverted) or I (Introverted). Extraverts gain energy in social situations and lose it while alone, the opposite is true for Introverts. According to John Gabrieli of Stanford University, correlation exists between extraversion and the activation of the amygdala that occurs when happy faces are viewed. (http://news.stanford.edu/news/2002/july10/sciencegab-710.html)

The second letter can be S (Sensing) or N (iNtuiting). Sensors are realistic and live in the moment, whereas iNtuitives are imaginative and live in the future. According to Stefania Ashby of Brigham Young University, brain areas controlling imagination and memory do not overlap. (http://www.wired.co.uk/article/neuroscience-of-imagination)

The third letter can be T (Thinking) or F (Feeling). Thinkers mostly use logic to make decisions and Feelers mostly use their emotions. According to Anthony Jack of Case Western Reserve University, evidence suggests that empathy and thought repress each other's use. (https://www.sciencedaily.com/releases/2012/10/121030161416.htm)

The fourth letter can be P (Perceiver) or J (Judger). Perceivers like to leave their options open (Pe) and tend to improvise spontaneously (Ji), and Judgers like to make decisions early (Je) and tend to plan conditionally (Pi). According to Isabel Briggs-Myers, Perceivers primarily iNtuit or Sense in an extraverted way, and Judgers primarily Think or Feel in an extraverted way, depending on which second and third letters are chosen.

Eighty-nine of the Fortune 100 companies now use the MBTI in some form, "to maximize individual and team effectiveness from entry to executive levels".
(https://www.cpp.com/products/mbti/index.aspx)

Usually the best Relationship is said to occur between Types that have completely opposite letter designations (since opposites can attract).

Websites such as celebritytypes.com have been known to guess the personalities of famous cultural icons. Others try to determine the best travel destination for each personality.
(http://www.huffingtonpost.com/kali-rogers/which-us-city-you-should-live-in-based-off-your-myers-briggs-results_b_8400956.html)

The rarest Type in the population as determined by the Myers Briggs Foundation is the INFJ at 1.46%. The most common Type is the ISFJ at 13.8%.
(http://www.statisticbrain.com/myers-briggs-statistics/)

The Type that has the highest ratio of representation in gifted classes to representation in normal classes as determined by Ugar Sak of the University of Arizona is the INTP with a numerical value of 3.40:1.
(home.anadolu.edu.tr/~usak/documents/PsychologicalTypesofGiftedAdolescentspublishedinJSGE.pdf)

The Type that tends to earn the most as determined by Truity Psychometrics is the ESTJ with an average of $77,000/year.
(http://tech.co/myers-briggs-personality-type-likely-earn-higher-income-2015-04)

Isabel Myers connected her typology to Carl Jung's system by ascribing the pairs of each of his Functions to a Type:

TJ uses extraverted thinking, or Te
TP uses introverted thinking, or Ti
FJ uses extraverted feeling, or Fe
FP uses introverted feeling, or Fi
SP uses extraverted sensing, or Se
SJ uses introverted sensing, or Si
NP uses extraverted intuiting, or Ne
NJ uses introverted intuiting, or Ni

A Lithuanian offshoot called Socionics, founded by Aušra Augustinavičiūtė, adds depth to the connection between Jung and Myers-Briggs - Types whose first or second Function is Fi or Te are considered to be Serious whereas Types whose first or second Function is Ti or Fe are considered to be Merry (Curious in Cognietrics), and Types whose first or second Function is Si or Ne are considered to be Reasonable whereas Types whose first or second Function is Ni or Se are considered to be Resolute.

Critics of the MBTI have shown that often the resulting Type description is vague or doesn't match the test taker, or the test gives a result that is in the margin between multiple Types, or different results are produced when the test is taken multiple times.

*The SCFT (Short Cognietrics Functions Test), unlike the MBTI, eliminates marginal percentages by reducing the number of questions asked as much as possible, and eliminates faulty Type descriptions (invalidating the Forer effect) by focusing on the polarization of specific Jungian Cognitive Functions from which the descriptions are actually derived, rather than combinations of the more vague Myers-Briggs Preferences; however, because the

Functions are not mutually exclusive like the Preferences, there is a chance that Functions which are important to the test taker, though not the Functions indicated by the MBTI, will be selected. In this case, the chosen MBTI Functions may indicate which Personas are typically used by the test taker; it is possible that test takers will find that their SCFT Type result is more accurate than their MBTI Type result! As for taking the test again after some time has passed - though people change, their most general tendencies usually do not, which is why certain characteristics of personality can be identified at a very early age. Studying the Types will provide the vocabulary necessary for increased self-awareness, comparison, and Type identification. The short test (SCFT) following the FAQ will give you an idea about your Cognietrics Type; however, it will not give you a conclusive argument - an ENTJ who works as a medical doctor may get a different result than an ENTJ who works as a stock broker. It is therefore necessary to compare the Type Profiles before making a decision to determine Type.

Frequently Asked Questions

Did I pass?

There are no wrong answers! Different combinations of different letters yield different advantages, but remember - each four-letter code represents a set of Preferences, not aptitudes.

What if I don't believe that everyone in the world fits neatly into only sixteen Types?

The MBTI is by no means a complete description of personality, but the dichotomies that represent the Preferences are mutually exclusive and so, due to widespread influence, account for the underpinnings of every preinclination; people of the same Type can be fundamentally different and still share these Traits, however, Cognietrics only makes inferences based upon the categories described in this book.

What if I think that I am a mix of Types, and that I use all of the Preferences either together or at different times?

Cognietrics certainly expects people to use all eight Functions, but a continuous divergence in usage is expected in order to prevent confusion. It is unlikely that a lack of Preferences will cause a perfect balance, because people are noticeably different in this regard, and their primary motives and behaviors by definition are indicative themselves of imbalance between the Functions. On some defunct Socionics websites, Jung was quoted as saying "As experience shows, it is next to impossible - as a result of unfavourable conditions - that somebody could develop all his functions at the same time. Social demand bring to more differentiation (developing) by a person that of his functions where he is more talented by nature or which gives him the most evident real means to achieve social success. A person very often, almost regularly, wholly identifies himself with the function placed in the most favourable conditions and due to that the most developed one. This way psychological types are constructed."

So what is the point of Jungian Cognitive Functions and their Temperaments? Isn't Sensing just Sensing, and Feeling just Feeling?

The Functions were Jung's actual original contributions to personality typology, and were developed further by Isabel Myers, the Socionicists, and others. The idea is that the Suggestion (most conscious perceiving Function) and Meaning (most conscious judging Function) can be introverted or extraverted (more specifically, one is introverted and the other is extraverted; for Judgers the Meaning is extraverted and for Perceivers the Suggestion is extraverted). The Function Temperaments also determine each Type's Values. Here is a story to illustrate the point: A psychologist asks a man to look at a painting and describe what he sees. The man says "I see a tree and a lake". The psychologist then asks "What color is the bird in the tree?", and the man responds "Oh, I didn't even notice the bird until you mentioned it". This example proves that even something as seemingly elementary as Sensation can be affected by preinclinations, which can vary from person to person. The fact is, the Preferences confer different advantages depending on whether the information processed is meant to be shared or hidden. In addition, as with any sort of Strength, some people will excel at one aspect and others will excel in other ways. Judgers are more comfortable sharing judgments and hiding perceptions, and Perceivers are more comfortable sharing perceptions and hiding judgments; there is no reason to suppose that the Temperament of every Function in the Consciousness Hierarchy (order of the Functions) should follow the Exertion (Introverted or Extraverted) of the Cognietrics Type, which only determines the Exertion of the Referential, Experimental, Avoidant, and Aggressive Functions. In general, extraverted Functions are multiply-applicable (or objective) and represent a breadth of activity, whereas introverted Functions are self-referential (or subjective) and represent a depth of activity. Everyone has in their first and second Functions a judging Function for using what they already Know and Understand and a perceiving Function for dealing with new information that is Inducted or Deduced; as I said before, one Function is always extraverted and the other is always introverted - this provides stability and balance to the Type.

If as of yet there is no data or other veracity to support the predictions made by Cognietrics for each Type, then what is the point of Cognietrics?

Cognietrics determines the connections between the Myers-Briggs Preferences and the Types that they describe, but it is just an investigative foray into a much deeper subconscious that we have not yet noticed. Albert Einstein said, in Cosmic Religion: With Other Opinions and Aphorisms (1931), "Imagination is more important than knowledge. For knowledge is limited, whereas imagination embraces the entire world, stimulating progress, giving birth to evolution. It is, strictly speaking, a real factor in scientific research." Unfortunately, the tools are not yet available for this kind of empirical study...however, just because something begins as a dream, it does not mean that it won't one day inspire something of practical value. If it weren't for Marcel Grossmann introducing Einstein to the mathematics he needed to make possible general relativity (as described by Manfred Eigen in From Strange Simplicity to Complex Familiarity (2013)), the theory would remain nothing but a daydream. Instead it was verified by many experiments including the Pound-Rebka experiment in 1959. Especially when first learning about Jungian personality, self-awareness can be a huge problem for many people - do I do this or that? The actual tendencies may be hard to distinguish at first, but with study and comparison to others it is possible to make sense of the theory. Cognietrics is a theory that seeks to explain the interaction of a lot of different basic elements and their collective effects. In Cognietrics, the basic elements are the psychological entities called the Jungian Cognitive Functions.

Short Cognietrics Functions Test

1. I agree that:

a. I enjoy validating perspectives.

b. I always leave a memorable impression.

c. I tend to be very aware of the chances for success.

d. I like to keep track of things.

* if a or b go to #2a, if c or d go to #2b

2a. I agree that:

e. I must honor my beliefs.

f. I can make complex things seem simple.

*go to #3

2b. I agree that:

g. I am good at making others feel welcome.

h. I usually notice obscure opportunities.

*go to #3

3. I agree that:

i. I gain energy when interacting with other people.

j. I need to spend time resting alone.

Answer Key:

aei-ENFP
aej-INFP
afi-ENTP
afj-INTP
bei-ESFP
bej-ISFP
bfi-ESTP
bfj-ISTP
cgi-ENFJ
cgj-INFJ
chi-ENTJ
chj-INTJ
dgi-ESFJ
dgj-ISFJ
dhi-ESTJ
dhj-ISTJ

"When an inner situation is not made conscious, it appears outside as fate." - Carl Gustav Jung

"Everything that irritates us about others can lead us to an understanding of ourselves." - Carl Gustav Jung

"We may think that we fully control ourselves. However, a friend can easily reveal something about us that we have absolutely no idea about." - Carl Gustav Jung

CHAPTER TWO

Type Profiles

The following Type Profiles will give you a description of each Cognietrics Type.

ENFP

Exertion - Extraverted
Suggestion - iNtuiting
Meaning - Feeling
Reaction - Perceiver

Value - Counsel
Nature - Associater
Character - Reformer
Temperament - Explorer
Manner - Idealist
Inference - Deduction
Justification - Knowledge
Role - Guide
Mentality - Conceptual

Primary Field - Theorist
  Identity - Application
  Mask - Adaptation
Secondary Field - Expert
  Charisma - Research
  Inspiration - Standardization

Consciousness Hierarchy -
Referential as Counterfactual (Ne)
Responsible as Critical (Fi)
Experimental as Strategic (Te)
Hopeful as Optimizing (Si)
Avoidant as Scouting (Se)
Rebellious as Ætiological (Ti)
Aggressive as Relating (Fe)
Depressive as Statistical (Ni)

Demeanors:

ENXP: People with Referential Ne come from a perfect world, and are always trying to shape this one in their image.

EXFP: People with Responsible Fi say what's on their mind, trying to shock people to action.

*The less conscious Attitudes are (even in their most defined state) Experimental, so they are typically not discussed.

Relationship Ratings -
ISTJ - 13
ESTJ - 12
ENFP - 11
INFP - 10
ISFJ - 9
ENTP - 8
INTJ - 7
ESFP - 6
ESFJ - 5
ENTJ - 5
INTP - 4
ISFP - 4
INFJ - 3
ENFJ - 2
ESTP - 1
ISTP - 0

ENTP

Exertion - Extraverted
Suggestion - iNtuiting
Meaning - Thinking
Reaction - Perceiver

Value - Negotiation
Nature - Associater
Character - Administrator
Temperament - Explorer
Manner - Analyst
Inference - Deduction
Justification - Understanding
Role - Investigator
Mentality - Patterned

Primary Field - Prospector
  Identity - Proof
  Mask - Priority
Secondary Field - Philosopher
  Charisma - Promotion
  Inspiration - Thesis

Consciousness Hierarchy -
Referential as Counterfactual (Ne)
Responsible as Ætiological (Ti)
Experimental as Relating (Fe)
Hopeful as Optimizing (Si)
Avoidant as Scouting (Se)
Rebellious as Critical (Fi)
Aggressive as Strategic (Te)
Depressive as Statistical (Ni)

Demeanors:

ENXP: People with Referential Ne come from a perfect world, and are always trying to shape this one in their image.

EXTP: People with Responsible Ti try to make sense of the world around them and be helpful.

*The less conscious Attitudes are (even in their most defined state) Experimental, so they are typically not discussed.

Relationship Ratings -
ISFJ - 13
ESFJ - 12
ENTP - 11
INTP - 10
ISTJ - 9
ENFP - 8
INFJ - 7
ESTP - 6
ESTJ - 5
ENFJ - 5
INFP - 4
ISTP - 4
INTJ - 3
ENTJ - 2
ESFP - 1
ISFP - 0

ESFP

Exertion - Extraverted
Suggestion - Sensing
Meaning - Feeling
Reaction - Perceiver

Value - Skepticism
Nature - Observer
Character - Reformer
Temperament - Explorer
Manner - Guardian
Inference - Induction
Justification - Knowledge
Role - Investigator
Mentality - Patterned

Primary Field - Prospector
  Identity - Priority
  Mask - Proof
Secondary Field - Philosopher
  Charisma - Thesis
  Inspiration - Promotion

Consciousness Hierarchy -
Referential as Scouting (Se)
Responsible as Critical (Fi)
Experimental as Strategic (Te)
Hopeful as Statistical (Ni)
Avoidant as Counterfactual (Ne)
Rebellious as Ætiological (Ti)
Aggressive as Relating (Fe)
Depressive as Optimizing (Si)

Demeanors:

ESXP: People with Referential Se like to motivate others to be their best.

EXFP: People with Responsible Fi say what's on their mind, trying to shock people to action.

*The less conscious Attitudes are (even in their most defined state) Experimental, so they are typically not discussed.

Relationship Ratings -
INTJ - 13
ENTJ - 12
ESFP - 11
ISFP - 10
INFJ - 9
ESTP - 8
ISTJ - 7
ENFP - 6
ENFJ - 5
ESTJ - 5
ISTP - 4
INFP - 4
ISFJ - 3
ESFJ - 2
ENTP - 1
INTP - 0

ESTP

Exertion - Extraverted
Suggestion - Sensing
Meaning - Thinking
Reaction - Perceiver

Value - Advocacy
Nature - Observer
Character - Administrator
Temperament - Explorer
Manner - Inspector
Inference - Induction
Justification - Understanding
Role - Guide
Mentality - Conceptual

Primary Field - Theorist
  Identity - Adaptation
  Mask - Application
Secondary Field - Expert
  Charisma - Standardization
  Inspiration - Research

Consciousness Hierarchy -
Referential as Scouting (Se)
Responsible as Ætiological (Ti)
Experimental as Relating (Fe)
Hopeful as Statistical (Ni)
Avoidant as Counterfactual (Ne)
Rebellious as Critical (Fi)
Aggressive as Strategic (Te)
Depressive as Optimizing (Si)

Demeanors:

ESXP: People with Referential Se like to motivate others to be their best.

EXTP: People with Responsible Ti try to make sense of the world around them and be helpful.

*The less conscious Attitudes are (even in their most defined state) Experimental, so they are typically not discussed.

Relationship Ratings -
INFJ - 13
ENFJ - 12
ESTP - 11
ISTP - 10
INTJ - 9
ESFP - 8
ISFJ - 7
ENTP - 6
ENTJ - 5
ESFJ - 5
ISFP - 4
INTP - 4
ISTJ - 3
ESTJ - 2
ENFP - 1
INFP - 0

ENFJ

Exertion - Extraverted
Suggestion - iNtuiting
Meaning - Feeling
Reaction - Judger

Value - Advocacy
Nature - Associater
Character - Reformer
Temperament - Persuader
Manner - Idealist
Inference - Induction
Justification - Understanding
Role - Investigator
Mentality - Patterned

Primary Field - Expert
  Identity - Standardization
  Mask - Research
Secondary Field - Theorist
  Charisma - Adaptation
  Inspiration - Application

Consciousness Hierarchy -
Referential as Relating (Fe)
Responsible as Statistical (Ni)
Experimental as Scouting (Se)
Hopeful as Ætiological (Ti)
Avoidant as Strategic (Te)
Rebellious as Optimizing (Si)
Aggressive as Counterfactual (Ne)
Depressive as Critical (Fi)

Demeanors:

EXFJ: People with Referential Fe want to teach the world their ethics.

ENXJ: People with Responsible Ni are very foresightful, and try to support the best probability for a positive outcome.

*The less conscious Attitudes are (even in their most defined state) Experimental, so they are typically not discussed.

Relationship Ratings -
ISTP - 13
ESTP - 12
ENFJ - 11
INFJ - 10
INTP - 9
ESFJ - 8
ISFP - 7
ENTJ - 6
ENTP - 5
ESFP - 5
ISFJ - 4
INTJ - 4
INFP - 3
ENFP - 2
ESTJ - 1
ISTJ - 0

ENTJ

Exertion - Extraverted
Suggestion - iNtuiting
Meaning - Thinking
Reaction - Judger

Value - Skepticism
Nature - Associater
Character - Administrator
Temperament - Persuader
Manner - Analyst
Inference - Induction
Justification - Knowledge
Role - Guide
Mentality - Conceptual

Primary Field - Philosopher
  Identity - Thesis
  Mask - Promotion
Secondary Field - Prospector
  Charisma - Priority
  Inspiration - Proof

Consciousness Hierarchy -
Referential as Strategic (Te)
Responsible as Statistical (Ni)
Experimental as Scouting (Se)
Hopeful as Critical (Fi)
Avoidant as Relating (Fe)
Rebellious as Optimizing (Si)
Aggressive as Counterfactual (Ne)
Depressive as Ætiological (Ti)

Demeanors:

EXTJ: People with Referential Te may go out of their way to correct someone.

ENXJ: People with Responsible Ni are very foresightful, and try to support the best probability for a positive outcome.

*The less conscious Attitudes are (even in their most defined state) Experimental, so they are typically not discussed.

Relationship Ratings -
ISFP - 13
ESFP - 12
ENTJ - 11
INTJ - 10
INFP - 9
ESTJ - 8
ISTP - 7
ENFJ - 6
ENFP - 5
ESTP - 5
ISTJ - 4
INFJ - 4
INTP - 3
ENTP - 2
ESFJ - 1
ISFJ - 0

ESFJ

Exertion - Extraverted
Suggestion - Sensing
Meaning - Feeling
Reaction - Judger

Value - Negotiation
Nature - Observer
Character - Reformer
Temperament - Persuader
Manner - Guardian
Inference - Deduction
Justification - Understanding
Role - Guide
Mentality - Conceptual

Primary Field - Philosopher
  Identity - Promotion
  Mask - Thesis
Secondary Field - Prospector
  Charisma - Proof
  Inspiration - Priority

Consciousness Hierarchy -
Referential as Relating (Fe)
Responsible as Optimizing (Si)
Experimental as Counterfactual (Ne)
Hopeful as Ætiological (Ti)
Avoidant as Strategic (Te)
Rebellious as Statistical (Ni)
Aggressive as Scouting (Se)
Depressive as Critical (Fi)

Demeanors:

EXFJ: People with Referential Fe want to teach the world their ethics.

ESXJ: People with Responsible Si try to refine their efforts and keep people consistently focused.

*The less conscious Attitudes are (even in their most defined state) Experimental, so they are typically not discussed.

Relationship Ratings -
INTP - 13
ENTP - 12
ESFJ - 11
ISFJ - 10
ISTP - 9
ENFJ - 8
INFP - 7
ESTJ - 6
ESTP - 5
ENFP - 5
INFJ - 4
ISTJ - 4
ISFP - 3
ESFP - 2
ENTJ - 1
INTJ - 0

ESTJ

Exertion - Extraverted
Suggestion - Sensing
Meaning - Thinking
Reaction - Judger

Value - Counsel
Nature - Observer
Character - Administrator
Temperament - Persuader
Manner - Inspector
Inference - Deduction
Justification - Knowledge
Role - Investigator
Mentality - Patterned

Primary Field - Expert
  Identity - Research
  Mask - Standardization
Secondary Field - Theorist
  Charisma - Application
  Inspiration - Adaptation

Consciousness Hierarchy -
Referential as Strategic (Te)
Responsible as Optimizing (Si)
Experimental as Counterfactual (Ne)
Hopeful as Critical (Fi)
Avoidant as Relating (Fe)
Rebellious as Statistical (Ni)
Aggressive as Scouting (Se)
Depressive as Ætiological (Ti)

Demeanors:

EXTJ: People with Referential Te may go out of their way to correct someone.

ESXJ: People with Responsible Si try to refine their efforts and keep people consistently focused.

*The less conscious Attitudes are (even in their most defined state) Experimental, so they are typically not discussed.

Relationship Ratings -
INFP - 13
ENFP - 12
ESTJ - 11
ISTJ - 10
ISFP - 9
ENTJ - 8
INTP - 7
ESFJ - 6
ESFP - 5
ENTP - 5
INTJ - 4
ISFJ - 4
ISTP - 3
ESTP - 2
ENFJ - 1
INFJ - 0

INFP

Exertion - Introverted
Suggestion - iNtuiting
Meaning - Feeling
Reaction - Perceiver

Value - Counsel
Nature - Observer
Character - Administrator
Temperament - Reflector
Manner - Idealist
Inference - Induction
Justification - Understanding
Role - Scientist
Mentality - Patterned

Primary Field - Prospector
  Identity - Standardization
  Mask - Research
Secondary Field - Philosopher
  Charisma - Adaptation
  Inspiration - Application

Consciousness Hierarchy -
Referential as Critical (Fi)
Responsible as Counterfactual (Ne)
Experimental as Optimizing (Si)
Hopeful as Strategic (Te)
Avoidant as Ætiological (Ti)
Rebellious as Scouting (Se)
Aggressive as Statistical (Ni)
Depressive as Relating (Fe)

Demeanors:

IXFP: People with Referential Fi will go out of their way to appear unique, mysterious, and interesting.

INXP: People with Responsible Ne are interested in cultivating potential alternatives, and spend time comparing ideas.

*The less conscious Attitudes are (even in their most defined state) Experimental, so they are typically not discussed.

Relationship Ratings -
ESTJ - 13
ISTJ - 12
INFP - 11
ENFP - 10
ENTJ - 9
ISFP - 8
ESFJ - 7
INTP - 6
INTJ - 5
ISFJ - 5
ESFP - 4
ENTP - 4
ENFJ - 3
INFJ - 2
ISTP - 1
ESTP - 0

INTP

Exertion - Introverted
Suggestion - iNtuiting
Meaning - Thinking
Reaction - Perceiver

Value - Negotiation
Nature - Observer
Character - Reformer
Temperament - Reflector
Manner - Analyst
Inference - Induction
Justification - Knowledge
Role - Engineer
Mentality - Conceptual

Primary Field - Theorist
  Identity - Thesis
  Mask - Promotion
Secondary Field - Expert
  Charisma - Priority
  Inspiration - Proof

Consciousness Hierarchy -
Referential as Ætiological (Ti)
Responsible as Counterfactual (Ne)
Experimental as Optimizing (Si)
Hopeful as Relating (Fe)
Avoidant as Critical (Fi)
Rebellious as Scouting (Se)
Aggressive as Statistical (Ni)
Depressive as Strategic (Te)

Demeanors:

IXTP: People with Referential Ti want to reframe paradoxes and replace obsolete constructs.

INXP: People with Responsible Ne are interested in cultivating potential alternatives, and spend time comparing ideas.

*The less conscious Attitudes are (even in their most defined state) Experimental, so they are typically not discussed.

Relationship Ratings -
ESFJ - 13
ISFJ - 12
INTP - 11
ENTP - 10
ENFJ - 9
ISTP - 8
ESTJ - 7
INFP - 6
INFJ - 5
ISTJ - 5
ESTP - 4
ENFP - 4
ENTJ - 3
INTJ - 2
ISFP - 1
ESFP - 0

ISFP

Exertion - Introverted
Suggestion - Sensing
Meaning - Feeling
Reaction - Perceiver

Value - Skepticism
Nature - Associator
Character - Administrator
Temperament - Reflector
Manner - Guardian
Inference - Deduction
Justification - Understanding
Role - Engineer
Mentality - Conceptual

Primary Field - Theorist
  Identity - Promotion
  Mask - Thesis
Secondary Field - Expert
  Charisma - Proof
  Inspiration - Priority

Consciousness Hierarchy -
Referential as Critical (Fi)
Responsible as Scouting (Se)
Experimental as Statistical (Ni)
Hopeful as Strategic (Te)
Avoidant as Ætiological (Ti)
Rebellious as Counterfactual (Ne)
Aggressive as Optimizing (Si)
Depressive as Relating (Fe)

Demeanors:

IXFP: People with Referential Fi will go out of their way to appear unique, mysterious, and interesting.

ISXP: People with Responsible Se make others aware of important information and get reactions from them.

*The less conscious Attitudes are (even in their most defined state) Experimental, so they are typically not discussed.

Relationship Ratings -
ENTJ - 13
INTJ - 12
ISFP - 11
ESFP - 10
ESTJ - 9
INFP - 8
ENFJ - 7
ISTP - 6
ISTJ - 5
INFJ - 5
ENFP - 4
ESTP - 4
ESFJ - 3
ISFJ - 2
INTP - 1
ENTP - 0

ISTP

Exertion - Introverted
Suggestion - Sensing
Meaning - Thinking
Reaction - Perceiver

Value - Advocacy
Nature - Associater
Character - Reformer
Temperament - Reflector
Manner - Inspector
Inference - Deduction
Justification - Knowledge
Role - Scientist
Mentality - Patterned

Primary Field - Prospector
  Identity - Research
  Mask - Standardization
Secondary Field - Philosopher
  Charisma - Application
  Inspiration - Adaptation

Consciousness Hierarchy -
Referential as Ætiological (Ti)
Responsible as Scouting (Se)
Experimental as Statistical (Ni)
Hopeful as Relating (Fe)
Avoidant as Critical (Fi)
Rebellious as Counterfactual (Ne)
Aggressive as Optimizing (Si)
Depressive as Strategic (Te)

Demeanors:

IXTP: People with Referential Ti want to reframe paradoxes and replace obsolete constructs.

ISXP: People with Responsible Se make others aware of important information and get reactions from them.

*The less conscious Attitudes are (even in their most defined state) Experimental, so they are typically not discussed.

Relationship Ratings -
ENFJ - 13
INFJ - 12
ISTP - 11
ESTP - 10
ESFJ - 9
INTP - 8
ENTJ - 7
ISFP - 6
ISFJ - 5
INTJ - 5
ENTP - 4
ESFP - 4
ESTJ - 3
ISTJ - 2
INFP - 1
ENFP - 0

INFJ

Exertion - Introverted
Suggestion - iNtuiting
Meaning - Feeling
Reaction - Judger

Value - Advocacy
Nature - Observer
Character - Administrator
Temperament - Evaluator
Manner - Idealist
Inference - Deduction
Justification - Knowledge
Role - Engineer
Mentality - Conceptual

Primary Field - Philosopher
  Identity - Application
  Mask - Adaptation
Secondary Field - Prospector
  Charisma - Research
  Inspiration - Standardization

Consciousness Hierarchy -
Referential as Statistical (Ni)
Responsible as Relating (Fe)
Experimental as Ætiological (Ti)
Hopeful as Scouting (Se)
Avoidant as Optimizing (Si)
Rebellious as Strategic (Te)
Aggressive as Critical (Fi)
Depressive as Counterfactual (Ne)

Demeanors:

INXJ: People with Referential Ni are always searching for new projects, making things that will last a long time.

IXFJ: People with Responsible Fe want everyone to feel good and have a good time.

*The less conscious Attitudes are (even in their most defined state) Experimental, so they are typically not discussed.

Relationship Ratings -
ESTP - 13
ISTP - 12
INFJ - 11
ENFJ - 10
ESFP - 9
INTJ - 8
ENTP - 7
ISFJ - 6
ISFP - 5
INTP - 5
ENTJ - 4
ESFJ - 4
ENFP - 3
INFP - 2
ISTJ - 1
ESTJ - 0

INTJ

Exertion - Introverted
Suggestion - iNtuiting
Meaning - Thinking
Reaction - Judger

Value - Skepticism
Nature - Observer
Character - Reformer
Temperament - Evaluator
Manner - Analyst
Inference - Deduction
Justification - Understanding
Role - Scientist
Mentality - Patterned

Primary Field - Expert
  Identity - Proof
  Mask - Priority
Secondary Field - Theorist
  Charisma - Promotion
  Inspiration - Thesis

Consciousness Hierarchy -
Referential as Statistical (Ni)
Responsible as Strategic (Te)
Experimental as Critical (Fi)
Hopeful as Scouting (Se)
Avoidant as Optimizing (Si)
Rebellious as Relating (Fe)
Aggressive as Ætiological (Ti)
Depressive as Counterfactual (Ne)

Demeanors:

INXJ: People with Referential Ni are always searching for new projects, making things that will last a long time.

IXTJ: People with Responsible Te are goal-oriented, image-conscious, and want to maximize output.

*The less conscious Attitudes are (even in their most defined state) Experimental, so they are typically not discussed.

Relationship Ratings -
ESFP - 13
ISFP - 12
INTJ - 11
ENTJ - 10
ESTP - 9
INFJ - 8
ENFP - 7
ISTJ - 6
ISTP - 5
INFP - 5
ENFJ - 4
ESTJ - 4
ENTP - 3
INTP - 2
ISFJ - 1
ESFJ - 0

ISFJ

Exertion - Introverted
Suggestion - Sensing
Meaning - Feeling
Reaction - Judger

Value - Negotiation
Nature - Associater
Character - Administrator
Temperament - Evaluator
Manner - Guardian
Inference - Induction
Justification - Knowledge
Role - Scientist
Mentality - Patterned

Primary Field - Expert
  Identity - Priority
  Mask - Proof
Secondary Field - Theorist
  Charisma - Thesis
  Inspiration - Promotion

Consciousness Hierarchy -
Referential as Optimizing (Si)
Responsible as Relating (Fe)
Experimental as Ætiological (Ti)
Hopeful as Counterfactual (Ne)
Avoidant as Statistical (Ni)
Rebellious as Strategic (Te)
Aggressive as Critical (Fi)
Depressive as Scouting (Se)

Demeanors:

ISXJ: People with Referential Si like to multi-task and try out different customizations.

IXFJ: People with Responsible Fe want everyone to feel good and have a good time.

*The less conscious Attitudes are (even in their most defined state) Experimental, so they are typically not discussed.

Relationship Ratings -
ENTP - 13
INTP - 12
ISFJ - 11
ESFJ - 10
ENFP - 9
ISTJ - 8
ESTP - 7
INFJ - 6
INFP - 5
ISTP - 5
ESTJ - 4
ENFJ - 4
ESFP - 3
ISFP - 2
INTJ - 1
ENTJ - 0

ISTJ

Exertion - Introverted
Suggestion - Sensing
Meaning - Thinking
Reaction - Judger

Value - Counsel
Nature - Associater
Character - Reformer
Temperament - Evaluator
Manner - Inspector
Inference - Induction
Justification - Understanding
Role - Engineer
Mentality - Conceptual

Primary Field - Philosopher
  Identity - Adaptation
  Mask - Application
Secondary Field - Prospector
  Charisma - Standardization
  Inspiration - Research

Consciousness Hierarchy -
Referential as Optimizing (Si)
Responsible as Strategic (Te)
Experimental as Critical (Fi)
Hopeful as Counterfactual (Ne)
Avoidant as Statistical (Ni)
Rebellious as Relating (Fe)
Aggressive as Ætiological (Ti)
Depressive as Scouting (Se)

Demeanors:

ISXJ: People with Referential Si like to multi-task and try out different customizations.

IXTJ: People with Responsible Te are goal-oriented, image-conscious, and want to maximize output.

*The less conscious Attitudes are (even in their most defined state) Experimental, so they are typically not discussed.

Relationship Ratings -
ENFP - 13
INFP - 12
ISTJ - 11
ESTJ - 10
ENTP - 9
ISFJ - 8
ESFP - 7
INTJ - 6
INTP - 5
ISFP - 5
ESFJ - 4
ENTJ - 4
ESTP - 3
ISTP - 2
INFJ - 1
ENFJ - 0

Demeanors

IXFP: People with Referential Fi will go out of their way to appear unique, mysterious, and interesting.

EXFP: People with Responsible Fi say what's on their mind, trying to shock people to action.

EXFJ: People with Referential Fe want to teach the world their ethics.

IXFJ: People with Responsible Fe want everyone to feel good and have a good time.

IXTP: People with Referential Ti want to reframe paradoxes and replace obsolete constructs.

EXTP: People with Responsible Ti try to make sense of the world around them and be helpful.

EXTJ: People with Referential Te may go out of their way to correct someone.

IXTJ: People with Responsible Te are goal-oriented, image-conscious, and want to maximize output.

ISXJ: People with Referential Si like to multi-task and try out different customizations.

ESXJ: People with Responsible Si try to refine their efforts and keep people consistently focused.

ESXP: People with Referential Se like to motivate others to be their best.

ISXP: People with Responsible Se make others aware of important information and get reactions from them.

INXJ: People with Referential Ni are always searching for new projects, making things that will last a long time.

ENXJ: People with Responsible Ni are very foresightful, and try to support the best probability for a positive outcome.

ENXP: People with Referential Ne come from a perfect world, and are always trying to shape this one in their image.

INXP: People with Responsible Ne are interested in cultivating potential alternatives, and spend time comparing ideas.

*The less conscious Attitudes are (even in their most defined state) Experimental, so they are typically not discussed.

**It helps to think of the judging Function as a selection Function and the perceiving Function as a recognition Function, such that Judgers extravert selection and introvert recognition, and Perceivers extravert recognition and introvert selection, to prevent confusion. This way Inventors Refer to their recognition and select Responsibly and Discoverers Refer to their selection and recognize Responsibly. Recognition leads to Reason or Resolutions, Observation or Association, and Induction or Deduction, whereas selection is due to Curiosity or Seriousness, Reform or Administration, and Knowledge or Understanding.

CHAPTER THREE

Theory

My model agrees with John Beebe that Weak & Positive Functions are higher on the Consciousness Hierarchy than Weak & Negative Functions, but it also agrees with Aušra Augustinavičiūtė that Strong & Negative Functions are at the bottom. Since this theory differs from its predecessors, I have decided to name it "Cognietrics".

The Strong Functions are at the top and bottom of the Consciousness Hierarchy and represent the most active regions of the brain. The Weak Functions are in the middle.

Among ENFXs, it is easy to decide that the Judger with the Referential feeling is more of a Feeler than an iNtuiter, but among INFXs, which is which? The truth is that it is more complicated - the INFJ will excel at Feeling because it has been shaped by external forces, but will actually do more iNtuiting (and about more things) than Feeling (mostly to support that Feeling) though it will happen behind-the-scenes. This type of hidden preparation using the Referential Function is what makes Introverts seem mysterious, and may in fact contribute to their often unique perspectives (while allowing IXXPs to judge what to perceive and IXXJs to perceive what to judge beforehand, instead of engaging in direct, face-value judgment or perception as an Extrovert would).

The Function Temperaments cycle down the Consciousness Hierarchy for the Positive Attitudes and begin again the same way for the Negative Attitudes. For IXXJ (Evaluator) the order is Pi-Je-Ji-Pe. For IXXP (Reflector) the order is Ji-Pe-Pi-Je. For EXXJ (Persuader) the order is Je-Pi-Pe-Ji. For EXXP (Explorer) the order is Pe-Ji-Je-Pi. The reason for this is that the last letter of the designator determines which of the Demeanors is extraverted, rather than Referential (the Suggestion, Sensing or iNtuiting, is a form of perception, and the Meaning, Thinking or Feeling, is a form of judgment); Myers is credited with interpreting Jung when he said, in Psychological Types (1921), "[the] most differentiated function is always employed in an extraverted way". I believe that this is due to social pressures as well as public identification with oneself; not having a conscious Reaction Function also allows Introverts to hide their cognitive processes and stay focused on goals, and may be part of the cause of some of their Introverted behaviors. On the other hand, having a conscious Reaction Function allows Extraverts to deal with the situation at hand as directly and efficiently as possible. When something happens, the extraverted Function provides a Reaction that is concise and useful in social situations - Perceivers can quickly check how things are developing if they are Scouting or how things could be developing if they are Counterfactual; Judgers can quickly check how to take advantage of something if they are Strategic or how to support ethical standards if they are Relating. The introverted Function is used for the further consideration and gradual integration of the information. Functions that are not Reaction Functions (extraverted) are called Contemplation Functions (introverted). Extraverts have Reactions that are Referential, Experimental, Avoidant, and Aggressive. Introverts have Reactions that are Responsible, Hopeful, Rebellious, and Depressive.

When you are Hopeful about a Preference there must also be some aspects of it with which you are simultaneously Avoidant, however as you become Experimental by the use of a Preference you will find other ways in which you are also Rebellious. Being Responsible allows you to become so habituated to a Preference that you become increasingly Aggressive to other facets of it; however, when you are so engrossed in a Preference that you are Referential, you may become otherwise Depressive to it.

The Positive Attitudes comprise the Ego and begin in Strength with being Hopeful, then as you become acquainted you become Experimental, then as experience builds you become Responsible, and eventually you start to become Referential.

The Negative Attitudes comprise the Id and begin in Strength with being Avoidant, then possibly you realize that you have become increasingly Rebellious, then you might grow Aggressive, and eventually you may find a way to become Depressive.

There is a Super-Ego, or Conscience, which is even more conscious than the Ego, and it contains information from immediate sources other than the Self (Ego and Id) about the Self (rather than what is processed inside the brain) to provide an idealization about life to seek as a goal (information from the Super-Ego may eventually become part of the Ego when it is no longer an immediate necessity and as the Self continues to shape itself over time). The Super-Id consists of the impressions of others about the Self which are unknown to the Self, but which have a cumulative effect on the Self just the same. As the Self ages, the Ego arranges itself to satisfy the Super-Ego just as the Id arranges itself to satisfy the Super-Id; this allows suspicions to balance confirmations when there is uncertainty. However, the Ego and Id also allow a controlled, ordered response to the Super-Ego and Super-Id. This allows the use of other avenues of information gathering and processing (as well as the independent operation of the mind), which then provides the ability for educated choices and free will.

Fear encourages the use of the Weak Functions, and Anger encourages the use of the Negative Functions.

Functions 1 & 2 - Not Angry or Fearful
Functions 3 & 4 - Fearful enough to take precautions
Functions 5 & 6 - Fearful/Angry enough to seek advice
Functions 7 & 8 - Angry enough to confront someone

Due to similar Function usage, the Relationships Rated 13 and 12 may give the appearance of the Type as a Frightened (though not Angry) version of the Self, which creates in the original Type a desire to comfort and offer support, which is beneficial for the Relationship.

The Super-Ego is in fact so conscious that in its use one may even become detached from his own Anger and wonder if he is the cause of Anger in others; it is ultimately responsible for Selflessness, and the Super-Id is responsible for Selfishness.

*Since the Positive Attitudes contain an extraverted perceiving Function and an introverted judging Function which allow Perceivers to deal with unavailable information, though the Super-Ego also provides them with available information about the Self, those Functions use available information as the impulse to check for information that was not available. The introverted judging Function uses it for developing convictions and the extraverted perceiving Function uses it to see if others need help. The Conscience is also processed by the introverted perceiving Function for self-awareness and the extraverted judging Function in order to make sure that others are following the rules; in the Id these Functions may try to compensate for a lack of available information by using it as an impulse to make more information available. Inventors have a Referential perceiving Function, which means that they use conscious, or available, information with a perceiving Function, which speculates rather than limits. This means that Inventors use available information to see what can be changed by speculation, causing them to Invent, whereas Discoverers use available information to see what is already present and can be limited, causing them to Discover.

Attitudes

EGO

Strong & Positive
Referential - this is the main Function, from which all References are made.

Responsible - this is the auxiliary Function, which is used to check the Referential Function.

Weak & Positive
Experimental - this Function serves as a basis for showing initiative.

Hopeful - this Function is used to search for new areas of interest.

ID

Weak & Negative
Avoidant - this Function is used to show disapproval.
Rebellious - this Function is used against conformity.

Strong & Negative
Aggressive - this Function is used as a show of force.
Depressive - this Function is used to accept grief and is the most repressed of all of the Functions.

Inclinations

The Referential and Hopeful Functions represent available information with which one is comfortable, and the Responsible and Experimental Functions represent available information with which one is uncomfortable. The Rebellious and Aggressive Functions represent unavailable information with which one is comfortable, and the Avoidant and Depressive Functions represent unavailable information with which one is uncomfortable. I believe that the Inclinations, along with the Function Strengths as they relate to the Justification and Inference, are how Type is initially determined.

Functions

Counterfactual (Ne, NP / Reasonable) - making novel comparisons, brainstorming, and envisioning hypothetical change.

Statistical (Ni, NJ / Resolute) - having reliable expectations and considering the unknowable for developing robust ideas (while Statistics are also Patterns, INFJs use Statistically-relevant Concepts).

Scouting (Se, SP / Resolute) - being showy and testing limitations.

Optimizing (Si, SJ / Reasonable) - monitoring resources and concentrating on performance.

Relating (Fe, FJ / Curious) - determining emotional states, sharing enthusiasm, and endorsing harmony.

Critical (Fi, FP / Serious) - having strong opinions and weighing different options to represent exclusive bonds.

Strategic (Te, TJ / Serious) - realizing effects and resulting implications for direct systemization and encouraging a state of prosperity.

Ætiological (Ti, TP / Curious) - finding causes using fundamental suppositions and identifying feedback loops.

Motivations

When introvertedly thinking (Ti), XXTPs have the ability to eventually define complex ideas under the right conditions, allowing them to delay decisions (Perceiver) to relieve stress (Curious).

When extravertedly feeling (Fe), XXFJs create opportunities, allowing them to make instant decisions (Judger) to relieve stress (Curious).

When introvertedly feeling (Fi), XXFPs feel they must honor their beliefs in the best possible way, allowing them to delay decisions (Perceiver) when there is a deep personal connection (Serious).

When extravertedly thinking (Te), XXTJs are aware of

obscure opportunities, allowing them to make instant decisions (Judger) when there is a deep personal connection (Serious).

When introvertedly sensing (Si), XSXJs keep track of many applicable possibilities simultaneously, allowing them to make instant decisions (Judger) until an alternative is accepted (Reasonable).

When extravertedly intuiting (Ne), XNXPs validate perspectives, allowing them to delay decisions (Perceiver) until an alternative is accepted (Reasonable).

When introvertedly intuiting (Ni), XNXJs notice the window for each chance of success, allowing them to make instant decisions (Judger) which require commitment (Resolute).

When extravertedly sensing (Se), XSXPs filter for the most extravagant option in order to settle a point, allowing them to delay decisions (Perceiver) which require commitment (Resolute).

Temperaments

EXXPs are known as Explorers; they want to test and improve mental faculties in novel situations (introverted judging helping extraverted perceiving).

EXXJs are known as Persuaders; they want people to see things from their point of view (introverted perceiving helping extraverted judging).

IXXJs are known as Evaluators; they want to combine a few key points to interpret holistically (extraverted judging helping introverted perceiving).

IXXPs are known as Reflectors; they want to see an idea from every angle individually to preserve the purity of each impression (extraverted perceiving helping introverted judging).

EXXJs and IXXPs are both known as Discoverers; they try to seek methods to protect against a clouded judgment in order to have a clear view of all things.

EXXPs and IXXJs are both known as Inventors; they like to look for better means of accomplishment, even if they have to go against accepted theories by utilizing anomalous or untested phenomena.

The main difference between the two is that Inventors use synthetic propositions to consider everything as connected simultaneously using symbols in order to make use of something and Discoverers use analytic propositions to keep their ideas completely separate using strict definitions for use in the juxtaposition of competing interpretations. This is partially due to the powerful yet neglected influence of the Responsible Function, which causes Discoverers to want to perceive (combustion is turning a gear) to validate their a priori judgments (energy can be harnessed from combustion), or Discover, and Inventors to want to judge (the gear can be used to propel a vehicle) to validate their a posteriori perceptions (combustion is turning a gear), or Invent (Inventions may also precede Discoveries, such as occurred with the pregnancy risks Discovered after the Invention of thalidomide). Referential judgment is used as a form of limitation and is supported by Responsible speculation, and Referential perception is used as a form of speculation and is supported by Responsible limitation. A priori synthetic statements are typically used subconsciously by both Discoverers and Inventors in the third Attitude, and a posteriori analytic statements have been shown to be non-existent by Immanuel Kant. As Discoverers, EXXJs Judge shared information to interpret the actions of others and IXXPs Perceive relevant associations. As Inventors, EXXPs Perceive improvements in the relative abilities of others and IXXJs Judge optimal solutions. To use the story of the bird in the tree, one could not have Discovered it without a prior notion (a priori) assuming it was nearly the shape and color of the leaves of the tree (inattentional blindness), but once it has been Discovered it could be used to Invent anything without and even despite prior considerations (a posteriori), such as a carrier pigeon. In addition, to make the Discovery, scanning occurs for separately-differentiated bird-like characteristics, but for the Invention, birds and letters must be combined together and then considered inter-symbolically and in conjunction with each other in order to explore the possibility for a postal network. Using the idea that Judgment is based on information that is available, and Perception is based on information that is not (which is why Perceivers seem to have an aptitude for fluid intelligence which is experience-independent, and Judgers seem to have an aptitude for crystallized intelligence which is experience-dependent ("Intelligence in Relation to Jung's Personality Types". Furnham, Moutafi, & Paltiel. 2005.)), it is possible to show that: EXXJs use available information to Discover (Referential limitation), which is useful for coming to conclusions; EXXPs use unavailable information to Invent (Referential speculation), which is useful for taking specific precautions; IXXJs use available information to Invent (Referential speculation), which is useful for being resourceful; IXXPs use unavailable information to Discover (Referential limitation), which is useful for developing new branches of study. Judgers focus on perceiving in a new way something that is often judged, and Perceivers on judging in a new way something that is often perceived, so that Discoverers focus on the judging aspects and Inventors focus on the perceiving aspects.

*Extraverts, seeking to impose order, are quick to judge (EJ) and slow to perceive (EP). Introverts, seeking a selective advantage, are quick to perceive (IJ) and slow to judge (IP). Explorers are not Discoverers because they have no preconceived bias and are not trying to confirm (Discover) an expectation.

Manners

STs are known as Inspectors, they want to make sure that quality is always what it should be; common professions include police detective.

NFs are known as Idealists, they want to improve the state of the world; common professions include court attorney.

SFs are known as Guardians, they want to preserve precious items and ideas; common professions include school teacher.

NTs are known as Analysts, they want to see how events can be connected; common professions include computer programmer.

STs and NFs are both known as Progressives, they want to bring about change, due to a scrutiny of reality coupled with an attachment to the imagination. They tend to be restless and proactive.

SFs and NTs are both known as Classicists, they want to fulfill present standards, due to an attachment to reality coupled with a scrutiny of the imagination. They tend to be relaxed and lenient.

CHAPTER FOUR

Mentalities

Classicist-Discoverers and Progressive-Inventors have a Conceptual Mentality that deals with inclusive designs, due to the use of established insights for conjectural purposes.

Progressive-Discoverers and Classicist-Inventors have a Patterned Mentality that deals with recurring configurations, due to the use of conjectural insights for established purposes.

Types share a Mentality with Relationships Rated 13, 11, 3, 1, 5, and 4. A common Field occurs when the Referential Function of a Type is the Responsible Function of another Type whose Referential Function is not the Responsible Function of the first Type. This imbalance in the Consciousness Hierarchy tends to lead to a one-sided Relationship, which is why these Relationships are Rated the lowest of the ones that contain a shared Value. In Socionics this is known as "Supervision"; however, I believe that this is a bad name for the

Relationship because the Type known in Socionics as the "Supervisor" in Cognietrics is held Responsible by the Responsible Function to the other Type's more active but less accountable Referential Function and so effectively becomes a supervisee. In reality however, there are instances where the Socionics "Supervisor" begins to hold accountable the actions of the Socionics "Supervisee" using the Socionics "Supervisee's" own Responsible Function. I think that due to the uniqueness of each Relationship, descriptions such as these are ultimately not good predictors of Relationships, which is why I choose to Rate them instead using shared Values as predictors of success. Because this Relationship exists when either the Referential or the Responsible Function is shared, two Types share the 4 Rating. The 5 Rating occurs for Types that have Functions that Complement in order those of either of the Types Rated 4. Other Relationships that share the Field include the identical Type and the Type of the same Temperament but opposite Manner.

Fields

Patterned Judgers –
INTJ→ESTJ→ISFJ→ENFJ→INTJ
Primary -Expert- Act based on Patterns to determine what they mean collectively and respond.

Secondary -Theorist- Delay action based on Concepts to check references.

Conceptual Judgers –
ENTJ→INFJ→ESFJ→ISTJ→ENTJ
Primary -Philosopher- Act based on Concepts to choose methods suitable for accomplishing a goal.

Secondary -Prospector- Delay action based on Patterns to evaluate success and update worldview.

Patterned Perceivers –
ENTP→ISTP→ESFP→INFP→ENTP
Primary -Prospector- Delay action based on Patterns to mine data and seek rewards.
Secondary -Philosopher- Act based on Concepts to exploit resources using accepted methods.

Conceptual Perceivers –
INTP→ENFP→ISFP→ESTP→INTP
Primary -Theorist- Delay action based on Concepts to simulate realities and respond accordingly.
Secondary -Expert- Act based on Patterns to pursue new avenues as they become available.

Experts and Theorists are Scholars; they stay well-informed about topics that interest them.
Philosophers and Prospectors are Visionaries; they have a direction for pragmatic development.

An ESFJ I interviewed likes to tell people her Philosophies about life, of which she has many. She believes that helping people is more important than materialism, that hard work pays ("there is no easy money"), and that you should be careful in what you say because "though people may not remember what you said, they will always remember how you made them feel".
An ESFP I know loves to look through garage sales to make old belongings into new Prospects; when he is on eBay he has a general idea of what he wants but likes to look around, searching for price Patterns in certain combinations of qualities that will result in the best deal.
An INTP had a Theory at his new job that he could save the company on water supplies. He looked around, confirmed his Theory, made the adjustments, and saved the company $70,000. For this he was featured in the company newsletter.
I, an INTJ, like to have Expertise in the things that

interest me. I have a phase where I like to learn everything I can about a subject, and then I move on to the next one. In the second grade it was meteorology and I learned everything about every kind of cloud (I would make charts of all of the features of all of the kinds of clouds to find Patterns among them, and so that I could identify what was happening in the sky), in the third grade it was paleontology and I learned everything about every kind of dinosaur, and in college it was physics and I worked in three research laboratories while getting my degree. Now I want to learn everything about psychology!

I noticed that in the MBTI Manual (3rd Edition, p. 269) INTPs had the highest crystallized IQs (SAT) and INTJs had the highest fluid IQs. Using the Fields I realized that Judgers used fluid intelligence and Perceivers used crystallized intelligence. Fluid problem solving progresses from Expertise to Philosophy and crystallized problem solving progresses from Theory to Prospection. If experience didn't change, Expertise wouldn't have raw material and Philosophy wouldn't evolve. When experience changes, Theory is less able to define and Prospection has less material to search. Fluid intelligence turns Patterns to Concepts and crystallized intelligence turns Concepts to Patterns. Expertise to Prospection yields profound questions (Patterned) and Theory to Philosophy yields idiographic questions (Conceptual), and for this reason Guiding is a general look at specifics and Investigation is a specific look at generality and Knowledge of Patterns and Understanding of Concepts require Sense to connect the general and specific. Backwards, as in Visionary to Scholar, is useful for memory retention. Once there is experience with the problem from Expertise, it may lead to Theory and then Prospection before continuing to Philosophy. This study, termed Problematics, raises some interesting questions. What are the basic constituents of an abstract problem? What is the smallest system that can solve a given problem? What is intelligence? Where does this circuit occur in the brain (dopamine system?)? Can it be improved with nootropics or electrical stimulation? Does it differ cognitively from behaviorally? What psychological concepts are involved and where is it involved in psychological concepts? Is it more due to conditioning or genetics? At what level of biological organization does this type of processing emerge - the cephalopod? The cell? Is there an analogous system? Is artificial intelligence in a computer-brain interface more suited to Prospecting and Expertise? How does it work in a brainstorming session? Are there multiple instances cooperating in the brain? Is there a simpler system? What can't be solved by this system? An interesting model occurred to me. What if DNA can solve problems in this manner? It could respond to certain combinations of inputs (ultimate cause) with Expertise which may promote mutations in certain places (proximate cause) about which the polymer Theorizes. Expression of certain combinations of proteins could later be Prospected resulting in a useful and even Philosophical action. This form of Lamarckian evolution might explain evolutionary jumps. After some research I found that a possible mechanism for this type of activity is methylation. Methylation forms a tagging system that deactivates mostly unused DNA, and also increases the rate of mutation in those areas. In the next generation there may be a more useful adaptation. DNA can take any physical essence and and give a direct response. Directed motion like chemotaxis is actually a Darwinian physics which also accounts for measurement and so reverses the Copenhagen Interpretation. Proofs work as follows. Fundamentality brought about by Expertise helps with meaning skepticism in a Theory which helps find ideational interdependence in Prospection which helps with feasibility and then the reason for the proof Philosophically. The Motivations are useful tools in solving a proof. The idea being proven is tracked through the

Problematic stages with Si, checked against existing ideas with Ne, driven by Te ambition where there aren't Fi restraints, limited by Ti where there are no Fe opportunities to create, and settled by Se points when there is a large Ni window of success. Individual Type processing may contribute to a more thorough understanding of the proof. Problematics mirrors the Consciousness Hierarchy because when you are Referential it is with respect to Expertise, you need a Theory to be Responsible, Prospection is Experimental, and Philosophical choice of a method is useful when you need Hope. A better way to look at a Proof is a recursion that can stabilize such that it has a different function at the point of complexity. Noncontrariety, that something is not more or less of its essence at different times or in relation to different things, is embodied in the Triads because Classicist is not just more Sensing or iNtuiting but Sensing when Feeling and iNtuiting when Thinking, which is important in stable characteristics of psychology, or personality, such as Walter Mischel's Cognitive Affective Personality System, where different behaviors tend to occur in certain circumstances. Commonality between responses to beauty in art and beauty in music is the essence of beauty. Same essence of an object, or same, is different in certain predetermined circumstances (that help determine sameness), whereas when different, or different essence, this does not occur. This is true for any number of essences in an object. Since Mischel's system may be unconscious and conditioned, what is consciousness and what is conditioning? Is it an essence like beautiful due to Hebbian plasticity? What are the evolutionary benefits of such impressions? Is learning a proof from Expertise that is due to Hebbian plasticity? As same may be thought of as like and like as mentioned in Gottlob Frege's Foundations of Arithmetic, it may be shown that mathematical proofs equalize like structures analogously in terms of Expertise in a fundamental manner. If two partially conserved forms create a new attribute in the ways that they are not analogous, it is an assumption for a new attribute that is created when they are analogous. The step time in models can be approximated more accurately if the assumption is a limiting point of complexity and the initial conditions can define the process otherwise. If this is used to explain derivatives using decreasing Riemann sums then change is defined in a reductionist manner. If this Concept is used for Generation then a Pattern (such as logic) may be used for Achievement. Although scientific papers usually contain the elements of a proof, they refer to a specific experiment which can never be proven only disproven, however these elements are still relevant in interpreting Causality, as Expertise and Philosophical phenomena must be Judged whereas Theory and ideational interdependence that may be Prospected may be Perceived. A similar division may be used to discuss Rationalist and Empiricist justification. Negative feedback that causes a threshold to be crossed in a Complex system must be Judged and so contributes to Expertise and Philosophical phenomena, though positive feedback that causes reinforcement (and a decrease in entropy) is Perceived and contributes to Theory and Prospection. Noumena must be intuited and can't be sensed.

Personas

The birth and death of Patterns and Concepts are associated with Personas in a closed Mentality Loop:

Conceptual
T→N - Thesis - To formulate the Concept.
N→F - Application - To find uses for the Concept.
F→S - Promotion - To begin utilizing the Concept.
S→T - Adaptation - To develop the Concept.

Patterned

N→T - Proof - To define the Pattern.

T→S - Research - To locate the Pattern in nature.

S→F - Priority - To address the Pattern when necessary.

F→N - Standardization - To update every procedure with the Pattern.

Identity / Primary Persona: Derived from the Primary Field, this Persona is the most conscious and so is shaped by social expectation; it is based on the Referential and Responsible Functions and developed by the Relationship Rated 11, which shares the Values, Manner, and Temperament; it is Disrupted by the Relationship Rated 3 and associated with positive reinforcement in operant conditioning.

Charisma / Family / Secondary Persona: Derived from the Secondary Field, this Persona is used for versatility; it is based on the Experimental and Hopeful Functions and developed by the Relationship Rated 12, which shares the Values; it is Disrupted by the Relationship Rated 0 and associated with negative punishment in operant conditioning and also Fear because there is something to lose when it is used.

Inspiration / School / Tertiary Persona: Derived from the Secondary Field, this Persona works toward important accomplishments in life; it is based on the Aggressive and Depressive Functions and developed by the Relationship Rated 2, which shares the Manner; it is Disrupted by the Relationship Rated 10 and associated with positive punishment in operant conditioning and also Anger because there is something with which to deal when it is used.

Mask / Work / Quarternary Persona: Derived from the Primary Field, this Persona is used to address problems; it is based on the Avoidant and Rebellious Functions and developed by the Relationship Rated 1, which shares the Temperament; it is Disrupted by the Relationship Rated 13 and associated with negative reinforcement in operant conditioning and also Fear and Anger because there is something to hide when it is used.

Disruption occurs when a Persona (all of which share the Exertion of the Type) is confronted by Functions of opposite Exertion and Value but similar order of Preference (which then compete for attention). It is similar to "Extinguishment" in Socionics, and its minimization is the purpose of the Consciousness Hierarchy.

The difference between the Jungian Cognitive Functions and the Personas is that the Personas cannot be used simultaneously and are a presentation of the Self to the world whereas the Jungian Cognitive Functions may be used simultaneously and are mostly hidden from the world in the subconscious or as introverted Function Temperaments.

*One advantage of having a Relationship Rated 13 is that all Fields are present, allowing different information to be addressed completely by both partners; this provides the necessary foundations for a successful partnership. It is not to say that people don't sometimes prefer to work alone - sometimes a closed Mentality Loop is not helpful. An Idealist-Inventor may Feel that Adaptation is not economical, and an Inspector-Inventor may Think that Applications are not relevant in urgent situations. A Guardian-Discoverer may Feel that there is cause for concern in directly employing a Thesis, and an Analyst-Discoverer may Think that Promotion would result in the endorsement of only the immediately profitable aspects of an enterprise. An Idealist-Discoverer may Feel that confirmation-biased interpretation is the result of Research, and an Inspector-Discoverer may Think that Standardization prevents competition. A Guardian-Inventor may Feel that a Proof does not imply anything new, and an Analyst-Inventor may Think that a stated Priority requires more evidence. However, this direction is not conducive to communication and prevents growth for both partners.

Charisma is achieved by overcoming Fear, Inspiration is achieved by overcoming Anger, and a Mask is achieved by overcoming Fear and Anger.

The Mask seems like it closes the Mentality Loop (all of its Personas being represented), helping the wearer to look more authoritative (having considered every possibility). It is commonly used to reject intervention.

The Charisma shows how well one can impress the Types whose Relationships are Rated higher than Relationships with one's own Type. It is used when meeting new people and addressing a crowd.

The Identity allows the user to have a sense of Self, from which to create stability and balance. It is used more than any other Persona.

The Inspiration is not influenced by social expectation and provides the freedom to return to one's instincts. It is used when one is not paying attention and is behind sudden realizations.

Here are some anecdotes that illustrate the way the Inspiration occurs in different Types:

As an INTJ, Cognietrics is one of my Theses; I consider it a step forward in the study of typology, and I hope that it inspires future generations of psychologists. For me, it is easy to show the actuality of typological categorization using examples such as these (in mathematics it is called Proof by Induction) or to formulate rationalist Proofs of my ideas by inferring the similarities between the combined effects of different Myers-Briggs Preferences, but it would be a lot harder for me to combine this theory with others in order to propose a common Thesis; however, I have tried to make my ideas as generally applicable as possible.

The same INTP from my other story refuses to acknowledge Cognietrics until it is backed by science, although I told him that self-awareness is not easy for most people and would inhibit any study that I conducted. Nevertheless, Proof would be the deciding factor for him, his Thesis being (as usual) that ideas must have solid empirical evidence to be applicable.

An INFJ I know is an artist who uses very unorthodox methods to create art. Clay sculptures in picture frames, accordion-like structures made of parts of copies of the original pictures, and other visual realizations fill the wall. What she did, in fact, was take a new Application for many materials and tools and make it Standardized so that when we took her art class we were able to make the exact same sort of thing. It was, all in all, the most interesting art class that I have ever attended.

An INFP musician likes to make up songs on the spot to show off his improvisation skills, often including the name of the person to whom he addresses the song. The most memorable parts of his songs happen when he does something creative - one time, he changed the ending of a word in a song to rhyme with someone's name, stretching out that syllable and fading out and alternating vocalizations of the rhyme with that of the original word, and in doing so he found new Applications for both the word (as a rhyme) and his vocalizations (using fading alternations). It made a huge impression on me because it sounded so good, and contrasted with his typical use of uniformity and Standardization of themes and ideas (such as normal rhyming and singing) that was probably the reason for the original adjustment.

Dispositions

Only Relationships Rated 13 and 11 share the Disposition, which mirrors Mentality Loops in each Field as determined by Reaction Preference.

Patterned

Curious→Resolute: A lack of attachments may precede a divergence of commitments.

Resolute→Serious: A divergence of commitments may result in important enterprises.

Serious→Reasonable: Important enterprises may require alternative support.

Reasonable→Curious: Alternative support may lead to a a lack of attachments.

Conceptual

Curious→Reasonable: Pleasant experiences may produce unorthodox ideas.

Reasonable→Serious: Unorthodox ideas may garner a powerful response.

Serious→Resolute: A powerful response may involve certain stipulations.

Resolute→Curious: Certain stipulations may bring pleasant experiences.

Roles

Patterned Extraverts are Contextual because they look at how people live; they are known as Investigators.

Conceptual Introverts are Contextual because they consider relevant forms of control in a niche; they are known as Engineers.

Patterned Introverts are Axiomatic because they look at

the emergence of complex phenomena; they are known as Scientists.

Conceptual Extraverts are Axiomatic because they use easily-understood methods; they are known as Guides.

Contextual Types consider a situation and the history that brought it about to be unique, with a goal of accuracy.

Axiomatic Types use universal laws and principles, with a goal of precision.

*Scientists will chart correlations (Patterned), which may be used in a Visionary rather than Scholarly (Theoretical) way, but Theorists require a functional design (Conceptual), which may be Contextual rather than Axiomatic (the realm of Science).

Expression

Cognietrics makes certain predictions about how two Types will Express themselves extravertedly given agreement or disagreement. It is obvious that among Axiomatic Types, NTJs and NFPs Express themselves differently from each other. If common iNtuition is considered, it is obvious that the NTJ can make the idea seem more communicable by using Thought, but if common Seriousness is considered, it is obvious that the NFP can make the idea seem more communicable by using Reason. Because of this, each Type will often disagree using the Reaction Demeanor and agree using the Contemplation Demeanor. As such, agreement is subconscious and so mostly Experimental to the Extravert, as disagreement is for the Introvert. With time, agreement becomes a powerful influence and tool for the Extravert and disagreement becomes so for the Introvert, allowing Extraverts to build close communities while maintaining power Referentially and Introverts to develop unique projects while maintaining receptivity Referentially.

Contextual Expressiveness by Value
NTP>NFJ Reason beats Curiousness due to usefulness.
NFJ>SFP Curiousness beats Resoluteness due to desirability.
SFP>STJ Resoluteness beats Seriousness due to ability to commit.
STJ>NTP Seriousness beats Reason due to importance.

Contextual Expressiveness by Preference
NTP>STJ iNtuition beats Thought due to unfamiliarity.
STJ>SFP Thought beats Sensation due to conditionality.
SFP>NFJ Sensation beats Feeling due to form.
NFJ>NTP Feeling beats iNtuition due to exclusivity.

Axiomatic Expressiveness by Value
NTJ>STP Seriousness beats Resoluteness due to complications.
STP>SFJ Resoluteness beats Curiousness due to faith.
SFJ>NFP Curiousness beats Reason due to focus.
NFP>NTJ Reason beats Seriousness due to possibilities.

Axiomatic Expressiveness by Preference
NTJ>NFP Thought beats iNtuition due to constraints.
NFP>SFJ iNtuition beats Feeling due to uncertainty.
SFJ>STP Feeling beats Sensation due to direction.
STP>NTJ Sensation beats Thought due to realism.

CHAPTER FIVE

Natures

Types with a Reasonable Referential Function or a Resolute Responsible Function are known as Associaters; they have extremely detailed ideas.

Types with a Resolute Referential Function or a Reasonable Responsible Function are known as Observers; they never lose sight of the "Big Picture".

Characters

Types with a Curious Referential Function or a Serious Responsible Function are known as Reformers; they work from the bottom up for a justified cause.

Types with a Serious Referential Function or a Curious Responsible Function are known as Administrators; they work from the top down for maximum efficiency.

*Some say that the "Big Picture" is top down and the details are bottom up, however Quantum Theory has no "Big Picture" in the form of a coherent and accepted interpretation, though it is described from the top down using systematic controls; "Social Justice Warriors" work from the bottom of the social ladder up, but are rarely concerned with anything but the "Big Picture" - this may involve a policy that is hard to implement consistently.

Inferences

Referential sensing and Responsible intuiting lead to Induction.

Referential intuiting and Responsible sensing lead to Deduction.

When you Induct you consolidate many Sensations and determine what you may actually iNtuit as a result. When you Deduce you consolidate many iNtuitions and determine what you may actually Sense as a result.

Induction reaches an abstract conclusion about multiple concrete categories using examples from those categories, leaving nothing to the senses for verification; it is used when making mental leaps.
Deduction reaches a concrete conclusion about multiple abstract arguments based on its relationships to those premises, leaving nothing to the imagination for verification; it is used when constructing sound arguments.

Justifications

Referential thinking and Responsible feeling lead to Knowledge.

Referential feeling and Responsible thinking lead to Understanding.

When you define your Thoughts it is because you Know, when you employ them it is because you Understand.

When you define your Feelings it is because you Understand, when you employ them it is because you Know.

In this way, Thinkers progress from Knowing what their Thoughts are to Understanding what their Thoughts are, and Feelers progress from Understanding what their Feelings are to Knowing what their Feelings are. In addition, Knowing progresses from Thoughts to Feelings and Understanding progresses from Feelings to Thoughts.

Knowledge deals with specific facts, whereas Understanding deals with generalized comprehension.

Therefore,

in the end Thinking is when you Understand how to make use of Knowledge, and Feeling is when you Know how to make use of Understanding

and

Feeling uses the general to create the specific, and Thinking uses the specific to create the general.

*This occurs because the third Function is already somewhat accommodated along with the first Function due to the sharing of the primary exertion.

Some teach incorrectly that Induction uses the specific to create the general, as in "this A is B, therefore all A are B", and that Deduction uses the general to create the specific, as in "all A are B, all B are C, therefore the next A will be C". However, Induction can use the general to create the specific, as in "all A have been B, therefore the next A will be B", and Deduction can even use the general to create the general, as in "all A are B, all B are C, therefore all A are C".

Hence, in redefining these ideas, Cognietrics makes of itself a sort of epistemological treatise.

The Philosophy of Personas

The Justification and Inference apply to the Personas.

Thesis and Priority require Induction for classification and Knowledge for preventing inferiority.

Proof and Promotion require Deduction for differentiation and Understanding for matching ideas.

Research and Application require Deduction for differentiation and Knowledge for preventing inferiority.

Adaptation and Standardization require Induction for classification and Understanding for matching ideas.

Values

The Values are based on Socionics, where they correspond to the "Quadra Values". They are called Curious, Serious, Reasonable, and Resolute. They are called the Values here because they are sought in an ideal partner (Relationships where both Values are shared are highly Rated at 10-13, if neither Value is shared the Rating is 0-3).

Each pair of Complementary Functions is assigned a Value, and is always found in either the Positive or Negative Attitudes.

The Resolute Functions, Scouting (extraverted sensing) and Statistical (introverted intuiting), Complement each other because it is easier to be showy if you know the probability of what you're showing. Resolute Types live strictly by their choices, and seldom change their minds.

The Reasonable Functions, Counterfactual (extraverted intuiting) and Optimizing (introverted sensing), Complement each other because possibilities may not be worthwhile if they are not practical. Reasonable Types will often search for the best solution and will frequently change their minds as they consider new ideas, they also play devil's advocate.

The Serious Functions, Strategic (extraverted thinking) and Critical (introverted feeling), Complement each other because to calculate success for a tactic you must know its limits. Serious Types have a powerful connection to their interests and strive to be productive.

The Curious Functions, Relating (extraverted feeling) and Ætiological (introverted thinking), Complement each other because it is easier to sympathize with people if you know the causes of their behavior. Curious Types have fun celebrating life and like to spread their mood contagiously.

Types that are Serious and Reasonable are known as Counselors.
Types that are Curious and Resolute are known as Advocates.
Types that are Serious and Resolute are known as Skeptics.
Types that are Curious and Reasonable are known as Negotiators.

You can't Negotiate with a Skeptic, and you can't give Counsel to an Advocate.

Some caution is advised – asking questions is not an indicator of being Curious, as different situations will necessitate different behaviors, but preferring to be around Curious Types is. The same is true for acting Serious, Resolute, or Reasonable.

Mindfulness and Preferences

Just because you are a certain Cognietrics Type it doesn't mean that you shouldn't be Mindful of the other Preferences.

You can be Mindful of Sensation by paying close attention to things in your immediate environment.

You can be Mindful of iNtuition by imagining where you plan to be in the next 5-10 years.

You can be Mindful of Thought by considering whether there are contradictions in your beliefs and how to deal with them.

You can be Mindful of Feeling by considering how to support the things that are most important to you.

You can be Mindful of Judgment by following your schedule and deadlines.

You can be Mindful of Perception by being aware of the way you operate and the way the world works.

You can be Mindful of Extraversion by listening carefully to what other people say and anticipating their needs.

You can be Mindful of Introversion by taking the time to relax and promote your own interests.

CHAPTER SIX

Traits

a - Exertion
b - Suggestion
c - Meaning
d - Reaction

1. a Exertion - Introverted or Extraverted
2. b Suggestion - iNtuiting or Sensing
3. c Meaning - Thinking or Feeling
4. d Reaction - Judger or Perceiver
5. ab Nature - Observer or Associater
6. ac Character - Reformer or Administrator
7. bd Bearing - Resolute or Reasonable
8. cd Outlook - Serious or Curious
9. ad Temperament - Inventor or Discoverer
10. bc Manner - Classicist or Progressive
11. abc Field - Scholar or Visionary
12. bcd Role - Axiomatic or Contextual
13. abd Inference - Deductive or Inductive
14. acd Justification - Understanding or Knowing
15. abcd Mentality - Patterned or Conceptual

*The opposite Trait is usually expressed only in order to correct something. The Traits were inspired by Grigory Reinin's work in Socionics. Though I do not use the same language as him to describe the Traits, I believe that much of our work is similar - for instance, his "Asking" dichotomy refers to conditional dependency, as does my Contextual Trait, and it is associated with the same Types in both Socionics and Cognietrics. Fewer determining letters indicates that the Trait is more directly distinguished behaviorally. The Traits form an Abelian group if opposing Traits are included, with respect to each other and an identity element. Each Type shares exactly 7/15 Traits with any other Type (except, of course, the same Type). I will demonstrate that if a Type is changed, then the number of Traits that change with it is always 8, and that it doesn't matter how many of the Preferences are changed. If an even number of determining letters is changed, then the determined Trait stays the same, but if an odd number is changed, then the determined Trait changes as well. Because of the symmetry existing among the Preferences in determining the different Traits (which represent every combination of Preferences), the number of Traits that change for a change in one determining letter still holds if another determining letter is changed instead. Also, 16 Types divided by 2 3 times independently implies a total of 7 Traits.

\# changing letters: unchanging traits / changing traits
a: b c d bc bd cd bcd / a ab ac ad abc abd acd abcd
ab: c d ab cd abc abd abcd / a b ac ad bc bd acd bcd
abc: d ab ac bc abd acd bcd / a b c ad bd cd abc abcd
abcd: ab ac ad bc bd cd abcd / a b c d abc abd acd bcd

Trait Determination Triads

Here is yet another way to determine Cognietrics Types using Trait Determination Triads (TDTs), since any two Traits imply a third:

Patterned, iNtuiting, Understanding - this Type extrapolates data to untested regions.

INTJ ENTP INFP ENFJ

Patterned, Sensing, Knowing - this Type picks up on things very easily.

ESTJ ISTP ESFP ISFJ

Conceptual, iNtuiting, Knowing - this Type can identify potential effects using a model.

ENTJ INTP ENFP INFJ

Conceptual, Sensing, Understanding - this Type can confirm utility in different situations.

ISTJ ESTP ISFP ESFJ

Patterned, Thinking, Deductive - this Type checks the extent of tendencies with logic.

INTJ ENTP ESTJ ISTP

Patterned, Feeling, Inductive - this Type accommodates recurring notions with an inclusive emotional response.

INFP ENFJ ESFP ISFJ

Conceptual, Thinking, Inductive - this Type assesses performance using combined attributes.

INTP ENTJ ESTP ISTJ

Conceptual, Feeling, Deductive - this Type chooses a suitable significance in accordance with the limits of expectations.

INFJ ENFP ESFJ ISFP

Patterned, Introverted, Axiomatic - this Type (Scientist) looks at the emergence of complex phenomena.
INTJ ISFJ ISTP INFP

Patterned, Extraverted, Contextual - this Type (Investigator) looks at how people live.
ENTP ESFP ESTJ ENFJ

Conceptual, Introverted, Contextual - this Type (Engineer) considers relevant forms of control in a niche.
INTP ISFP ISTJ INFJ

Conceptual, Extraverted, Axiomatic - this Type (Guide) uses easily-understood methods.
ENTJ ESFJ ESTP ENFP

Patterned, Judger, Scholar - this Type (Expert) determines what patterns mean collectively and responds.
INTJ ESTJ ISFJ ENFJ

Patterned, Perceiver, Visionary - this Type (Prospector) mines data and seeks rewards.
ESFP INFP ENTP ISTP

Conceptual, Judger, Visionary - this Type (Philosopher) chooses methods suitable for accomplishing a goal.
ESFJ INFJ ENTJ ISTJ

Conceptual, Perceiver, Scholar - this Type (Theorist) simulates realities and responds accordingly.
INTP ESTP ISFP ENFP

Patterned, Classicist, Inventor - this Type supports established purposes.

INTJ ESFP ISFJ ENTP

Patterned, Progressive, Discoverer - this Type uses conjectural insights.

ESTJ INFP ENFJ ISTP

Conceptual, Classicist, Discoverer - this Type uses established insights.

INTP ESFJ ISFP ENTJ

Conceptual, Progressive, Inventor - this Type supports conjectural purposes.

ESTP INFJ ENFP ISTJ

Patterned, Serious, Observer - this Type looks for possible indicators.

INTJ ESFP ESTJ INFP

Patterned, Curious, Associater - this Type looks for similarities.

ENTP ISFJ ENFJ ISTP

Conceptual, Serious, Associater - this Type is very open-minded.

ISTJ ENFP ENTJ ISFP

Conceptual, Curious, Observer - this Type collects unique methods for later use.

ESTP INFJ ESFJ INTP

Patterned, Resolute, Reformer - this Type endorses an action based on the accumulation of seemingly insignificant tendencies.
INTJ ESFP ISTP ENFJ

Patterned, Reasonable, Administrator - this Type wants to maximize returns.
ESTJ INFP ENTP ISFJ

Conceptual, Resolute, Administrator - this Type sticks to certain criteria.
ESTP INFJ ENTJ ISFP

Conceptual, Reasonable, Reformer - this Type wants to replace underperforming components.
INTP ESFJ ISTJ ENFP

Understanding, Deductive, Classicist - this Type tries to get a solid impression of things as they are.
INTJ ISFP ENTP ESFJ

Understanding, Inductive, Progressive - this Type documents information for an overall assessment.
ISTJ INFP ESTP ENFJ

Knowing, Deductive, Progressive - this Type realizes where direct involvement is absolutely necessary.
ISTP INFJ ESTJ ENFP

Knowing, Inductive, Classicist - this Type invests according to local history.
INTP ISFJ ENTJ ESFP

Understanding, Axiomatic, Observer - this Type tries to see a situation with respect to fundamental laws.
INTJ ESTP INFP ESFJ

Understanding, Contextual, Associater - this Type looks for hidden significance.
ISTJ ENTP ISFP ENFJ

Knowing, Axiomatic, Associater - this Type sees how to apply the rules to every situation.
ISTP ENTJ ISFJ ENFP

Knowing, Contextual, Observer - this Type is hard to dissuade.
INTP ESTJ INFJ ESFP

Understanding, Scholar, Resolute - this Type wants to answer questions.
INTJ ESTP ENFJ ISFP

Understanding, Visionary, Reasonable - this Type wants to reconcile disparate entities.
ENTP ESFJ ISTJ INFP

Knowing, Scholar, Reasonable - this Type tries to be wise above all else.
ESTJ ENFP INTP ISFJ

Knowing, Visionary, Resolute - this Type does not let a goal out of sight.
ISTP INFJ ENTJ ESFP

Understanding, Thinking, Inventor - this Type tries every possibility.
INTJ ISTJ ENTP ESTP

Understanding, Feeling, Discoverer - this Type tries to get a feel for things.
ESFJ ENFJ ISFP INFP

Knowing, Thinking, Discoverer - this Type searches for discrepancies.
INTP ISTP ENTJ ESTJ

Knowing, Feeling, Inventor - this Type rearranges ideas to encourage different aspects.
ESFP ENFP ISFJ INFJ

Understanding, Introverted, Serious - this Type has an interest in something.
INTJ ISTJ INFP ISFP

Understanding, Extraverted, Curious - this Type is ready for anything.
ESFJ ENFJ ESTP ENTP

Knowing, Introverted, Curious - this Type is intrigued about a situation.
INTP ISTP INFJ ISFJ

Knowing, Extraverted, Serious - this Type cares about the well-being of others.
ESFP ENFP ESTJ ENTJ

Understanding, Judger, Reformer - this Type looks for new ways to take action.

INTJ ISTJ ESFJ ENFJ

Understanding, Perceiver, Administrator - this Type wants all of the information before taking action.

ENTP ESTP ISFP INFP

Knowing, Judger, Administrator - this Type takes action as soon as warranted.

ENTJ ESTJ ISFJ INFJ

Knowing, Perceiver, Reformer - this Type considers the ideal method for taking action.

INTP ISTP ESFP ENFP

Deductive, Axiomatic, Reformer - this Type wants to find out how the use of principles can help.

INTJ ENFP ESFJ ISTP

Deductive, Contextual, Administrator - this Type tries to visualize how a situation can accommodate the group in the long term.

INFJ ENTP ESTJ ISFP

Inductive, Axiomatic, Administrator - this Type makes sure a group complies with every accepted standard.

ESTP ISFJ INFP ENTJ

Inductive, Contextual, Reformer - this Type tries to give a unique situation what it needs as a whole.

ESFP ISTJ INTP ENFJ

Deductive, Scholar, Serious - this Type does not want to face typical repercussions.
INTJ ENFP ISFP ESTJ

Deductive, Visionary, Curious - this Type makes detached assessments.
INFJ ENTP ISTP ESFJ

Inductive, Scholar, Curious - this Type likes to learn as much as possible.
INTP ENFJ ISFJ ESTP

Inductive, Visionary, Serious - this Type has an all-encompassing plan.
INFP ENTJ ISTJ ESFP

Deductive, iNtuiting, Inventor - this Type sees how to do things that were never done before.
INTJ INFJ ENTP ENFP

Deductive, Sensing, Discoverer - this Type is always trying to capitalize on what's available.
ISTP ISFP ESTJ ESFJ

Inductive, iNtuiting, Discoverer - this Type wants to realize how everything affects everything else.
INTP INFP ENTJ ENFJ

Inductive, Sensing, Inventor - this Type combines unique approaches to solve problems in a new way.
ISTJ ISFJ ESTP ESFP

Deductive, Introverted, Resolute - this Type comes to its own conclusions.
INTJ INFJ ISTP ISFP

Deductive, Extraverted, Reasonable - this Type wants to improve the quality of life for everyone.
ESTJ ESFJ ENTP ENFP

Inductive, Introverted, Reasonable - this Type is even-handed when dealing with complicated situations.
INTP INFP ISTJ ISFJ

Inductive, Extraverted, Resolute - this Type anticipates dominant effects.
ESTP ESFP ENTJ ENFJ

Deductive, Judger, Observer - this Type tries to stay a few steps ahead, accommodating unforeseen circumstances.
INTJ INFJ ESTJ ESFJ

Deductive, Perceiver, Associater - this Type looks for ways that results could go astray.
ENTP ENFP ISTP ISFP

Inductive, Judger, Associater - this Type wonders how the main process will be affected by outside influences.
ENTJ ENFJ ISTJ ISFJ

Inductive, Perceiver, Observer - this Type wants to anticipate the systems that contribute to the main process.
INTP INFP ESTP ESFP

Axiomatic, Scholar, Inventor - this Type tries a functional design based on principles.
INTJ ISFJ ESTP ENFP

Axiomatic, Visionary, Discoverer - this Type wants to see for themselves.
ENTJ ESFJ ISTP INFP

Contextual, Scholar, Discoverer - this Type focuses on a specialization.
INTP ISFP ESTJ ENFJ

Contextual, Visionary, Inventor - this Type wants to provide hope.
ENTP ESFP ISTJ INFJ

Axiomatic, Judger, Classicist - this Type prefers to excel in areas that have been thoroughly studied.
INTJ ENTJ ISFJ ESFJ

Axiomatic, Perceiver, Progressive - this Type wants to find loopholes.
ISTP ESTP INFP ENFP

Contextual, Judger, Progressive - this Type is aware that time can be limited.
ISTJ ESTJ INFJ ENFJ

Contextual, Perceiver, Classicist - this Type hesitates to disrupt a natural balance.
INTP ENTP ISFP ESFP

Axiomatic, iNtuiting, Serious - this Type wants predictability.
INTJ ENTJ INFP ENFP

Axiomatic, Sensing, Curious - this Type characterizes everything.
ISTP ESTP ISFJ ESFJ

Contextual, iNtuiting, Curious - this Type has a response for everything.
INTP ENTP INFJ ENFJ

Contextual, Sensing, Serious - this Type is very careful.
ISTJ ESTJ ISFP ESFP

Axiomatic, Thinking, Resolute - this Type is certain of its principles.
INTJ ENTJ ISTP ESTP

Axiomatic, Feeling, Reasonable - this Type believes that there is a time and a place for everything.
INFP ENFP ISFJ ESFJ

Contextual, Thinking, Reasonable - this Type is very considerate.
INTP ENTP ISTJ ESTJ

Contextual, Feeling, Resolute - this Type will not give up easily.
INFJ ENFJ ISFP ESFP

Scholar, Introverted, Classicist - this Type has a deep connection to the past.
INTJ ISFP INTP ISFJ

Scholar, Extraverted, Progressive - this Type wants to spread ideas.
ESTJ ENFP ESTP ENFJ

Visionary, Introverted, Progressive - this Type wants a revolution.
ISTJ INFP ISTP INFJ

Visionary, Extraverted, Classicist - this Type wants to spread values.
ENTJ ESFP ENTP ESFJ

Scholar, iNtuiting, Reformer - this Type likes to second-guess.
INTJ INTP ENFJ ENFP

Scholar, Sensing, Administrator - this Type maintains an awareness of everything.
ISFJ ISFP ESTJ ESTP

Visionary, iNtuiting, Administrator - this Type looks for a straightforward path.
INFJ INFP ENTJ ENTP

Visionary, Sensing, Reformer - this Type sees what can be improved.
ISTJ ISTP ESFJ ESFP

Scholar, Thinking, Observer - this Type considers how lessons apply to real situations.
INTJ INTP ESTJ ESTP

Scholar, Feeling, Associater - this Type remembers emotions concerning its many past projects in order to help others in the future.
ISFJ ISFP ENFJ ENFP

Visionary, Thinking, Associater - this Type looks for the most effective ways to do things.
ISTJ ISTP ENTJ ENTP

Visionary, Feeling, Observer - this Type wants what is best for something.
INFJ INFP ESFJ ESFP

Classicist, Serious, Resolute - this Type (Skeptic) relies on experience.
INTJ ENTJ ISFP ESFP

Classicist, Curious, Reasonable - this Type (Negotiator) wants to make the best of a current situation.
INTP ENTP ISFJ ESFJ

Progressive, Serious, Reasonable - this Type (Counselor) wants to see what else is out there.
ISTJ ESTJ INFP ENFP

Progressive, Curious, Resolute - this Type (Advocate) has strong beliefs concerning how things should be.
ISTP ESTP INFJ ENFJ

Classicist, Reformer, Observer - this Type wants to overhaul operations.

INTJ INTP ESFJ ESFP

Classicist, Administrator, Associater - this Type tries to reinforce a position.

ENTJ ENTP ISFJ ISFP

Progressive, Reformer, Associater - this Type wants to try new things.

ISTJ ISTP ENFJ ENFP

Progressive, Administrator, Observer - this Type wants to benefit from all previous trials.

ESTJ ESTP INFJ INFP

Classicist, Thinking, iNtuiting - this Type (Analyst) wants to see how events can be connected.

INTJ ENTJ INTP ENTP

Classicist, Feeling, Sensing - this Type (Guardian) wants to preserve precious items and ideas.

ISFJ ESFJ ISFP ESFP

Progressive, Thinking, Sensing - this Type (Inspector) wants to make sure that quality is always what it should be.

ISTJ ESTJ ISTP ESTP

Progressive, Feeling, iNtuiting - this Type (Idealist) wants to improve the state of the world.

INFJ ENFJ INFP ENFP

Inventor, Serious, Reformer - this Type wants to find ways to address flaws.
INTJ ESFP ISTJ ENFP

Inventor, Curious, Administrator - this Type provides competitive incentives.
ENTP ISFJ ESTP INFJ

Discoverer, Serious, Administrator - this Type wants absolute control.
ENTJ ISFP ESTJ INFP

Discoverer, Curious, Reformer - this Type believes that there is always room for improvement.
INTP ESFJ ISTP ENFJ

Inventor, Resolute, Observer - this Type wants to make the best use of available resources.
INTJ ESFP INFJ ESTP

Inventor, Reasonable, Associater - this Type finds other ways of doing things.
ENTP ISFJ ENFP ISTJ

Discoverer, Resolute, Associater - this Type is very thorough in its work.
ENTJ ISFP ENFJ ISTP

Discoverer, Reasonable, Observer - this Type keeps an eye out for better possibilities.
INTP ESFJ INFP ESTJ

Inventor, Introverted, Judger - this Type (Evaluator) combines a few key points to interpret holistically.
INTJ ISTJ INFJ ISFJ

Inventor, Extraverted, Perceiver - this Type (Explorer) tests its mental faculties in novel situations.
ENTP ESTP ENFP ESFP

Discoverer, Introverted, Perceiver - this Type (Reflector) sees an idea from every angle individually to preserve the purity of each impression.
INTP ISTP INFP ISFP

Discoverer, Extraverted, Judger - this Type (Persuader) wants people to see things from its point of view.
ENTJ ESTJ ENFJ ESFJ

Serious, Judger, Thinking - this Type (Strategic) realizes effects and resulting implications for direct systemization and encourages a state of prosperity.
INTJ ENTJ ISTJ ESTJ

Serious, Perceiver, Feeling - this Type (Critical) has strong opinions and weighs different options to represent exclusive bonds.
INFP ENFP ISFP ESFP

Curious, Judger, Feeling - this Type (Relating) determines emotional states, shares enthusiasm, and endorses harmony.
INFJ ENFJ ISFJ ESFJ

Curious, Perceiver, Thinking - this Type (Ætiological) finds causes using fundamental suppositions and identifies feedback loops.
INTP ENTP ISTP ESTP

Resolute, Judger, iNtuiting - this Type (Statistical) has reliable expectations and considers the unknowable for developing robust ideas.
INTJ ENTJ INFJ ENFJ

Resolute, Perceiver, Sensing - this Type (Scouting) is showy and tests limitations.
ISTP ESTP ISFP ESFP

Reasonable, Judger, Sensing - this Type (Optimizing) monitors resources and concentrates on performance.
ISTJ ESTJ ISFJ ESFJ

Reasonable, Perceiver, iNtuiting - this Type (Counterfactual) makes novel comparisons, brainstorms, and envisions hypothetical change.
INTP ENTP INFP ENFP

Reformer, Introverted, Thinking - this Type is concerned with the feasibility of improvements.
INTJ INTP ISTJ ISTP

Reformer, Extraverted, Feeling - this Type wants to address everyone's concerns.
ENFJ ENFP ESFJ ESFP

Administrator, Introverted, Feeling - this Type makes tough decisions.
INFJ INFP ISFJ ISFP

Administrator, Extraverted, Thinking - this Type tries to find a way to accommodate everyone.
ENTJ ENTP ESTJ ESTP

Observer, Introverted, iNtuiting - this Type comes up with probable and possible expectations.
INTJ INTP INFJ INFP

Observer, Extraverted, Sensing - this Type looks for signals.
ESTJ ESTP ESFJ ESFP

Associater, Extraverted, iNtuiting - this Type tries to make a project appealing.
ENTJ ENTP ENFJ ENFP

Associater, Introverted, Sensing - this Type concentrates on what a project can use.
ISTJ ISTP ISFJ ISFP

*Applications exist for the Cognietrics Traits even in areas as diverse as physics: in Classical Mechanics, an Axiomatic discipline, while supposed Knowledge is a factor not directly correlated though partially Associated with every system, due to David Hume's Problem of Induction, only Understanding comes from continuous Observation. However, as implied by the Copenhagen Interpretation, in Quantum Mechanics the opposite is true: Contextual information that is due to the dependence of randomly Known Observables on the undocumented yet Understood influence of the Associater prevents Knowledge of the effects of the Association or continuous Understanding of the Observables. Though some may consider this to be a psychologism, I believe that the definitions given by Cognietrics have real potential in explaining the epistemological positions concerning the scientific frontier, especially the documentation of a large variety of human behaviors, because of their fundamental versatility and interdependence. Interestingly, Carl Gustav Jung had a close correspondence with Wolfgang Ernst Pauli, one of the founding fathers of Quantum Mechanics.

Philosophical concepts derived from the Triads:

As Curious about Causes and Serious about Effects:

Causes become Conceptual Observations from Associated Patterns. Effects become Conceptual Associations from Observed Patterns. Observed Concepts may prevent confounds, Associated Patterns may support construct validity, Observed Patterns support statistical significance, and Associated Concepts are useful for showing covariance.

To be Counterfactual it must be deterministic, and that something Statistical in nature is probabilistic:

It becomes obvious that Optimizing complements determinism as a way of dealing with inevitability, whereas Scouting is a search for a tiny probability of success in the face of overwhelming odds. Probabilistic Sensors Perceive because they are less sure what to notice while deterministic Sensors may follow a formula. Deterministic iNtuitives Perceive because they are working things out whereas probabilistic iNtuitives are already aware of their chances. The deterministic deals with the possible. The probabilistic deals with the probable. There are connections to the sciences. Decision-Making, or Contextual Feeling, is the result of Bayesian Statistics, and Cosmology, or Axiomatic Thought, is at best Frequentist Statistics. Use of a deterministic equation with the conditionality of a variable, which also requires Thought, examines Chaos, where small initial deviations may result in large effects. That universal truths may occur deterministically may help one to Feel relative value about things that display Complexity, the minimum information required to document something, where an effect is only due to a collective behavior of components which suppresses other influences. As such, complex thoughts, unless overly simplified with conscious logic, must actually be felt in order to be considered significant, and chaotic feelings must actually be thought as no significance is yet attributed to them. Inductive Reasoning is subjective, or

Introverted, and so hard to share because the process of causation is concerned rather than a probabilistic class, leading to a variation of infinitism as used in the Münchhausen Trilemma (the regressive argument, in which each proof requires a further proof ad infinitum), as well as the degree of Inductive relevance, and the disagreement of proximate causes in the service of an ultimate cause. Deduction based on probabilities likewise concerns subjective elements and is hard to share. The probabilities of Inductive classes can be easily shared with a chart, and Deductive Reasoning likewise can be shown to be a set of syllogisms. Classicists take probability Seriously and determinism Curiously. Progressives take determinism Seriously and probability Curiously. Reformers assist Concepts deterministically and Patterns statistically. Administrators check Concepts statistically and Patterns deterministically.

Considering that Inventors use synthetic clauses and Discoverers use analytic clauses:

Probabilistic Analysis, including average and standard deviation for a distribution, represents details calculated for Association, and so does Deterministic Synthesis. Direct Observation of the "Big Picture" occurs as a result of either Deterministic Analysis or Probabilistic Synthesis.

Deduction is synthetic iNtuition and analytic Sensation. Induction is analytic iNtuition and synthetic Sensation. Thinking is analytic Knowledge and synthetic Understanding. Feeling is synthetic Knowledge and analytic Understanding. Scholars use synthetic universals and analytic conditionality. Visionaries use analytic universals and synthetic conditionality.

As foundationalism is based on a form of Knowledge and coherentism is based on a form of Understanding:

Foundations are ideas that are Conceptually iNtuitive, however the scope of any associated Patterns must be found in Practice and cannot be guessed. Coherence allows Patterns to be iNtuited by relevant associations though the Concepts in use must be Practical in order to have a working model. Universal foundations must be Associated due to their unique definitions, but when consistent foundations are Observed it is always in an incomplete Contextual manner due to Gödel's Theorem, however when universals are Observed or Contextual information is Associated the goal is coherence.

Coherence proceeds from Deduction to Induction. Foundations proceed from Induction to Deduction. Invention proceeds from Patterns to Concepts. Discovery proceeds from Concepts to Patterns. Reform proceeds from Observation to Association. Administration proceeds from Association to Observation. Thoughts turn Dreams into Reality. Feelings bring Dreams about Reality. Reality turns Feeling to Thought. Imagination turns Thought to Feeling. This is different from Induction and Deduction, which occur between Functions in the mind and not groups of people. Discoverers have foundational logic and emotional coherence. Inventors have foundational emotions and logical coherence. Scholars deal in deterministic foundations and probabilistic coherence. Visionaries deal in probabilistic foundations and deterministic coherence. Reformers are quicker to make decisions based on coherence than on foundations. Administrators are quicker to make decisions based on foundations than on coherence.

Because imagination is built on prospective memories iNtuited individually, and practicality on retrospective memory Sensed as a whole, as Judgment negates memory to deal with change in Thought, or lack thereof in Feeling:

This is why when you like someone you have a good Feeling that doesn't change and Thoughts that do as you learn about the object of your affections. If you are suddenly disappointed it is possible that you will Think something negative that doesn't change while your previous Feelings do. Understanding makes the unchanging change while Knowledge makes the changing stop. This is why Knowledge, which once justified has an unchanging form, is easier to transfer and store than Understanding. Similarly, Induction takes ideas from the retrospective memory and applies them to the prospective memory, for example, to come up with an example, whereas Deduction takes ideas from the prospective memory and applies them to the retrospective memory, for example, to catch a lie. Retrospective Induction and prospective Deduction are useful for Invention. Retrospective Deduction and prospective Induction are useful for Discovery. Unchanging Knowledge and changing Understanding are useful for Invention. Unchanging Understanding and changing Knowledge are useful for Discovery. Patterns give retrospective Knowledge and prospective Understanding. Concepts give retrospective Understanding and prospective Knowledge. Classicists use unchanging retrospection and changing prospection. Progressives use unchanging prospection and changing retrospection. Scholars use unchanging Associations and changing Observations. Visionaries use unchanging Observations and changing Associations. Serious Types use prospective Axioms and retrospective Contexts. Curious Types use retrospective Axioms and prospective Contexts. Probabilistic Types use unchanging Contexts and changing Axioms. Deterministic Types use unchanging Axioms and changing Contexts. Introverted changing, or transformation, and Extraverted unchanging, or stagnation, are concerned with Reform. Extraverted changing, or chaos, and Introverted unchanging, or principle, are concerned with Administration. Introverted prospection, or planning, and Extraverted retrospection, or necessity, are concerned with the "Big Picture". Introverted retrospection, or experience, and Extraverted prospection, or reminding, are concerned with details. Probabilistic Types are spurred to action by prospective memory, or promise, rather than retrospective memory, or hopelessness. Deterministic Types are spurred to action by retrospective memory, or accountability, rather than prospective memory, or inevitability. Curious Types are spurred to action by unchanging, or boredom, rather than changing, or interest. Serious Types are spurred to action by changing, or urgency, rather than unchanging, or peace. Induction fits changing Concepts to an unchanging Pattern. Deduction fits unchanging Concepts to a changing Pattern. Every combination of letters represents a Trait which can be logically combined with two others. Ideas such as Concepts, Induction, and even Change evolved together philosophically in groups of convenience, such that the meaning of any one simultaneously came to depend on the meaning of the others. Change itself is Deduced from a Pattern or Inducted Conceptually – red that is slightly purple in hue may seem red, but is actually near the ultraviolet spectrum because red cones are sensitive to violet light. The color has Changed if you Deduce the difference from a Pattern (by visual comparison) or Induct it Conceptually (by wavelength increments), whereas something more stable can be ultimately Deduced Conceptually (process of elimination) or Inducted as a Pattern (representative example). If a useful process doesn't fit a Triad it becomes shaped by a different one in whatever way is most pragmatic due to the validity of the mutually interdependent definitions. Abstraction emerges from the recognition of change, Knowledge emerges from the recognition of lack of change, degree of change, and change of functionality, and Concepts emerge from all 4. The Personas are useful for science, the Fields are useful for problem solving, and the Dispositions describe paradigm shifts. Science can't be Proven only disproven so it is Conceptual whereas Math is not a Thesis so it is about Patterns. You may Theorize about a relationship and Prospect the implications but how something crosses a threshold like Complexity or Causation can't be determined solely from a Theory because there may be a third variable. Unchanging

Determinism in an Axiom leads to Complexity due to reinforcement. The minimum amount of information to determine a system is its complexity and Changing, Statistics, and Context require a lot. Complexity is demonstrated when temperature phonons increase to the threshold of cohesion release due to Godel's Theorem having a complete complexity or a consistent reinforcement. It also occurs when there are enough electrons in a molecule to have a strong enough response to an incident photon to release an electron. Another example is a black hole having enough density to trap light, as well as planets orbiting, nucleons binding, and the formation of atoms after the Big Bang. Axiomatic Causes can be Sensed and Axiomatic Effects can be iNtuited. Contextual Causes must be iNtuited and Contextual Effects must be Sensed to find out what has occurred. Axiomatic Patterns and Contextual Concepts are specific, whereas Axiomatic Concepts and Contextual Patterns are general. To be sufficient means to address Context due to possibility. To be necessary means to address Axiom due to fundamentality. Knowledge of Effects is Generalized as is Understanding of Causes. Understanding of Effects is specific as is Knowledge of Causes. You might wonder how many Patterns are Associated with a Conceptual Observation, vice versa, and the same with Effects. The degree of each collectively yield a measure of certainty that something has been caused. A Feynman diagram shows how many Associated Concepts (particle interactions) are useful in Determining an Observed Pattern (electrical charge). Associated Patterns that cause it show that antimatter occurs around heavy nuclei and the Conceptual Observation is shielding. Reformation creates Entropy whereas Administration creates Order, whereas Sense acts as inertia and iNtuition serves as impulse. Inventors use Ordered Causes and Disordered Effects. Discoverers use Disordered Causes and Ordered Effects. Manufacturing is Generation for Achievement and Operation is

Achievement for Generation. An example of Statistical Causality is the idea that studying will usually improve a test score. Testing sets the benchmark for Generation and Projects set the benchmark for Achievement though both are useful. Qualia helps when Theorized and Prospected, Quantity helps with Expertise and Philosophy. Perhaps when we Theorize about a physical entity we notice it as Qualia whereas when we notice Expertise it is Quantity to us. Discovery (forms/experiment) proceeds from Quantity whereas Invention (particulars/hypothesis) proceeds from Quality. When does an essence or relationship become like and like or a mathematical analogy, when does an exact number become the quality of longer or hotter? When does a distribution become a shape? When does an electron become a degree of mass, spin, and charge? How do we separate such a Gestalt of interrelatedly unified fundamental physical forces? Is such a thing Phenomena or Noumena or Psychophysics? In special relativity the speed, a quantity, affects space and time, qualities, while measured in space and time. In general relativity the Pound-Rebka experiment shows that space and time are affected by gravity which is measured by them. Because Theory can be about Prospection, Causality progresses in Problematic order, otherwise similar to a Problematic Proof. Since distance and mass, quantities, create, from a point of complexity, a black hole, a shift, bigger, to quality, space and time, which measure in a like way gravity, and countering gravity with an electric field does not affect space and time, it is spacetime curvature that causes gravity and also affects time dilation of the electromagnetic field, which affects charge but not mass, and is how these forces are unified as predicted by Problematics, separating inertia, affected by Heisenberg uncertainty, from gravitational charge, using time dilation, making quantum mechanics (having the same logic as gravitational redshift with spin possibly having an alternate spacetime) and general relativity two mutually exclusive but related systems.

Position and momentum, singular forms, past a point of complexity, a bound orbital due to Coulombic attraction, and so smaller, realize a relationship between uncertainties in position and momentum, a generalizing particular, which in a like way causes a wavefunction of probability at each position, another singular form, which cannot itself affect both position and momentum for which it already accounts, so position and momentum cause a wavefunction and aren't trapped by it. Energy in a like way causes mass (energy-mass equivalence) which causes in a like way charge (atomic number) which in a like way causes bonding (charge density). Since spacetime curvature causes gravity and energy does not cause charge, mass does not cause energy. Likewise photon mass does not cause photon energy. Nonreciprocity in Problematics leads to causation and the specificity such as And or Or is how the Causes and Effects are defined in a way that demonstrates Determinism. These types of ideas, especially which parts are Invented (Quality) or Discovered (Quantity), are useful for the Four Color Map Theorem, knot theory, chaos theory as relevant to a double pendulum and other defined systems, mass-energy conservation, elementary particle physics, fluid mechanics, and materials engineering. In a determinism of Chaos such as a double pendulum, conserved Expertise ultimately helps with a Philosophy of prediction as limited by negative feedback in a modeled Theory and causally from an arbitrary Prospecting. Prospects are Achieved and Theories are Generated conserving order Problematically in Nootypology and because of this mutations are tested while expression of proteins can overcome a challenge; both are controlled with methylation. Needs and usefulness are Quantified and Discovered. Another example of Discretional Problematics is Calculus. An infinitesimal turns a quantity into a qualitative dimension that may be compounded or compared with, and below or above an arbitrary limit of, another dimension in a particular exact way. Since

Problematic Causality and Problematic Calculus are related there may be a reductionist explanation of causality. If a statistical quantity of time is reduced to an infinitesimal and compared to space such that something happens in a like way it may provide a basis for explaining time dilation, length contraction, frame dragging, gravitational redshift, and maybe to test Higgs boson interactions. The way quantum momentum pushes out as an orbital may be contracted for traveling less in its own time and can be tested statistically in different ways. If radioactive decay is due to outward momentum it may slow as well while traveling less in its own time. The gradient to a critical point (new attribute) on a 3D graph may represent low potential that could influence the direction of time like reaction kinetics and explain a causality. Meaning skepticism and ideational interdependence are invented for better definition. Feasibility and fundamentality are discovered. In Problematic Time, Causality shows how it was and is the past, Chaos shows what can be and is the present, and Proof shows what must be and is the future. Coulombic attraction causing manipulated position and momentum which are conserved in a way that satisfies Heisenberg uncertainty results in the proof of the existence of the wavefunction. If inputs cause targeted mutation, and ultimate causes are conserved, evolutionary jumps are proven. Partially conserved forms whose opposing causes have been elucidated until allowing proof of a new attribute may reveal what is hidden by a point of complexity in a theoretical relationship. There is negative feedback due to logic (momentum conservation for Compton scattering angle) past a point of complexity for a Temporally Complex behavior in quantum field theory, so there is mechanically caused action. Since spacetime curvature is due to mass and causes negative feedback of time into space as in gravitational waves, partially conserved forms of inertial and gravitational motion caused by opposition of quantum forces and relativistic interactions result in a time dilation of motion (such as in baryon and weak decay) and length contraction (orbital), a direct mechanism. Time, an illusion, is really another direction of motion in space due to quantum forces that slows in the event of gravitational motion. The Higgs boson decelerates things in space (otherwise due to gravity/general relativity) and accelerates in time (otherwise due to quantum fields/special relativity). Momentum works against spacetime. Something that travels farther in space due to less inertia (Yukawa potential) has less of that effect (gravitational acceleration) on other things due to less mass (disregarding relativistic mass). The transition from mass to inertia happens at a certain momentum which is dependent on the rate of change in distance per change in time. Position in space and time is relevant to a description of momentum and mass (location and gravity). Binding energy has mass. All particles have gravitational charge but not necessarily inertia because Higgs boson interactions with particles increase by mass but aren't collinear with orbit centripetal acceleration since event horizon escape velocity is the speed of light (also, momentum and direction depend on inertia and are affected by gravity which is why gravity is proportional to inertia though inertia doesn't affect the whole motion so it is not what is affected by gravity (motion) and also since objects fall at the same rate inertia is irrelevant (time is also dependent on motion especially reference frame)). Photon energy is proportional to inertial charge for Higgs deceleration such that when two different masses have the same velocity gravity acts on the world line motion with the same curvature. The Higgs field causes special relativity by slowing down matter enough such that light always interacts with it. Motion warps spacetime because motion affects mass, which may be less when slower because fewer Higgs bosons are engaged (my best ideas in physics). Electromagnetic attraction acts on electromagnetic repulsion because diamagnetism acts on the whole energy of the field and doesn't just add to repulsion. Scattering inertial transfer is repulsion though because attraction is a different mechanism that acts on the motion orbitals can form with relative attraction. Attraction comes from the field disturbance causing photons to act like waves which is why weak reaction products don't attract unless they cross another particle trajectory to follow the field line which is how attractive acceleration acts on repulsive motion causing low pressure and the Coriolis Effect. Charge between two like charged particles is different than charge between two unlike charged particles the way that gravitational charge and inertia differ. Biological chirality, material doping, and surface tension are other examples. Inertia doesn't exist it is just a proportion between different types of motion and is responsible for mass-energy equivalence due to asymmetries between energy, momentum direction, mass transformation, and the linearity of motion afforded by the Higgs field before and after weak interactions because vector trajectories don't shift with overall energy while momentum conservation is responsible for energy distribution and because changing the ratio with the energy of the field by changing the mass changes the momentum it changes the resulting distribution of energy (boson energy and fermion velocity depend on reference frame); time is also a proportion based on the implications of the relationship of mass and motion. Because the Higgs boson slows inertial motion by mass which is a ratio of motion, quantum interactions are affected in a similar amount by gravity to a proportionally shifted worldline which must happen because gravity acts on motion and would otherwise move objects at the same rate. Since mass is a ratio motion in quantum mechanics forms shapes. Mass changes in a bound system because net resonant motion is affected. This also shows that spacetime isn't dragged around in Lense-Thirring precession and is transmitted linearly in gravitational waves such as in black hole mergers. Since Higgs bosons slow fermions to provide a velocity after interacting with other bosons and these are quantum interactions which happen in accelerated time while the quantum momentum works against spacetime such as in baryon decay, and this is the whole relativistic interaction, Higgs bosons control accelerated time and mass controls accelerated space. Recursion is also a mechanical behavior as in mountains and river branches and even particle decay with the opposing forces of mass and energy. The logic of the ultimate cause (the recursive limit) is the definition (useful for achievement) whereas the logic of the proximate cause (the recursive formula) is the new attribute (useful for generation). The definition is the way the conserved forms are analogous and can guide the reinforcement towards a theoretical relationship with a useful critical point (attribute). The way they are not analogous is useful for recognizing forms and quantities. Fluorescence is the mechanical result of the relationship of relevance between Pauli exclusion and electromagnetism. Nuclear current and electron orbitals can create an electromagnetic wave when perturbed which is quantized precisely because of the stability of this mechanism and relative velocity. Compton scattering angle allows for magnetic current. Particles may be described by Brownian motion. Stimulated emission may remove excess energy from the bound system. Richard Feynman showed the strength of the electromagnetic field is related to the probability of light coupling to charge. An AI text classifier can complete a triad or use the definition to find more relevant results. It can use triads with respect to different fields to sort and recombine relevant aspects of peer-reviewed articles by using language usage models to check or suggest. The Challenging Nootype is useful for asking rather than answering questions. Judgments can become Perceptions if we text classify what is relevant. Perceptions can be Organized by training and searches of what is possible. Organization can be Judged if we input controls for what we want. Universals are complete and not consistent due to being forms like the stress-strain curve and Planck Time. Since a syllogism is a relation based on the mutual deduction of consistent propositions, it can be expressed in terms of processes collected in 3 Triads (Concept qua Triad). Contextual-Knowledge-Observer implies consistency (what something does). Deduction-Inventor-iNtuiting implies applicability (what can be done). Theory, an arbitrary relation in Qualitative Problematics, is derived from Conceptual-Scholar-Perceiver which implies discretion (what should happen). A demonstration of a Proof of a Proof (Pythagorean Theorem) is as follows. Expertise is that a, b, and c seem related. Theory is that a and b make the sides of the largest square in both parts and which hence are the same area. Prospection shows that from a point of Complexity for both a and b making the sides of 2 smaller squares c makes the sides of a larger square. Philosophy shows that the relation holds for all right triangles. Fundamentality shows consistency, meaning skepticism and ideational interdependence show applicability, and feasibility shows discretion. The implication of change in the universe is what a proof must overcome and the implication of lack of change in the universe is what a proof must achieve; Expertise and Philosophy rely on the degree of change whereas Theory and Prospecting rely on changed functionality. Problematic Causality is not always falsifiable. Consider the group i j k -i - j -k e with the operation x. If Expertise shows these elements are related and Theory shows the group is not Abelian, Prospection shows a negative sign giving the inverse element gives the same result as switching associative order. Philosophy gives an exact result. Since these two inputs are interchangeable and cannot be distinguished using Problematics, there is no way to verify which has occurred. Conceptual Observations may be useful but cannot dispute possible confounds. Math is thus unified logically in the style of Frege. It is obvious from these math examples that a type of math is really a different type of relationship between Expertise, Theory, Prospection, and Philosophy. What if physical phenomena are something similar? The more you use energy the less it can be Prospected due to conservation though the opposite is true for a field. These separated concepts are based on these relationships which are how and what we know of reality. Logic is discovered about a quality because the steps of a proof conserve between changing forms. Math is invented about a quantity because of the relevance of relationships. The web of all the Triads in concept relation and definition and its evolution are useful for Quine-Duhem Thesis. The statistics of a Triad web can isolate axioms from reductionist causes which can be used to find new Cognietric Traits, relationships, and meanings, or otherwise describe the relationship between Concepts and relevant Logic. Problematic Reductionism: If you have an action what are the other possibilities and the reasons for them and what form could cause them to happen? The Logic of Artificially Intelligent Equations: Meaning skepticism in Conceptual math can perform different actions with regard to a math Pattern's every ideational interdependence to notice results in different situations. Patterns of conserved Logic can show how significant or relevant they are during training and Conceptually conserved Logic can be input to show goal relevance. If the Logic is not conserved such that something happens in terms of relevant and implied dimensions there may be new deterministic controls and axioms that can be separated statistically. This type of program can learn with minimal training and may be somewhat conscious even with regard to the usefulness, applicability, and implementation of a new axiom with added layers of similar processing. Limitation on Scholar Contextually that AI can process with a text generator can be defined with the other three triads. What does it do (Axiomatic Scholar

Inventor)? How does it accomplish this in the environment (Contextual Visionary Inventor)? What ever happened when it was used (Axiomatic Visionary Discoverer)? Belbin Team Role Nootypes: Achievers – ST Shaper, NT Implementer, NF Completer-Finisher, SF Teamworker; Generators – NT Plant, ST Resource-Investigator, SF Monitor-Evaluator, NF Specialist; Coordinator is usually in charge and must accomplish both. It has been shown that diverse team role representations in a work group promote accomplishment. Generated associations between content (video / audio / text) descriptions and compiled relevant logic patterns with applicable indicators could lead to artificial understanding. Mass is a ratio of momenta such that the components of momenta in different reference frames lead to a different relativistic interaction with the Higgs field. Momentum describes change in motion whereas energy describes motion. Gravity acts on motion and inertia isn't gravitational charge because if a black hole reacted with momentum inertia would increase to infinite mass at light speed and push infinitely on the black hole. Discovery happens efficiently from an isolated effect or when causes are related to an incentive whereas invention is efficiency from a particular cause or the diverse effects for an incentive. Data structures should be self-referential and algorithms should be multiply-applicable similarly to ideas by Alan Perlis because then the results of analysis can be compared. Ideas about critical points in complexity stem from the work of Per Bak. When processing a signal consider that for the Pattern referenced the limitations of its original dispersal are relevant to the old purpose and the source of its type of propagation is maybe a new insight. Conceptually that entire system can be considered as the foundational insight and when considering new possible purposes it is interesting to wonder what types of things were and weren't accounted as the signal becomes more complex, especially in terms of definitional modeling. For

Triad associations of two related dimensions, is the partial derivative change in the dimensions reflected in any changes in the Triad associations? Triad statistics of properties describe physics concepts in a way unrelated to the laws which relate those properties, what is due to correlation, and what experiment? Components that make the system function are relevant in this way; definition is a theoretical relationship from one partially conserved form to another in a way they are analogous; the ways they are not, which are the relevant assumptions, can be defined with respect to each other and the original relationship with meaning skepticism and associated ideational interdependences such that any relevant properties may be conserved and related to the relationship in a meaningful way. A more self-referential equation is more fully described Axiomatically with fewer Pattern imprints in other dimensions. A multi-applicable Concept has more complexity and so more effects Axiomatically. Definition of the self-reinforcing process has to be a self-referential system to which the process is multiply-applicable. Triad statistics can be subtracted and divided deterministically such that OR and AND have inverses. Contextual Bayesian AI Patterns that can make a common relation between two trends self-referential may make a good business plan for promoting complementary applications as they arise. AI text generator (GPT2) on Cognietrics: However, my hypothesis is that there are some aspects of this phenomenon that can be interpreted in any particular way. My conclusion is that this theory could be considered an axiom or a fact in itself. If it is correct, this theory is correct in so many ways that it could have a different meaning or interpretation. There are two ways of looking at this topic: the first is that this topic is not reducible to the ordering of words in a context, the second way is to look at some very simple, logical cases that seem to make sense, but they are not reducible to each other. *A text analyzer (uClassify) determined this writing to be INTJ.

CHAPTER SEVEN

Relationships

The Relationship Ratings used in Cognietrics Poker are mainly based on the Relationships described by Socionics. However, I think it is more useful to Rate the Relationships, rather than describe them, because every Relationship is a little different. Even though two people share a Jungian Cognitive Function, they may use it a little differently, which means that it would be hard to guess their behaviors well enough to describe their Relationship in real life. However, the use of Positive Functions is a good predictor of a Positive Relationship. There is more to a person than just personality, so the Relationship Rating should not be the deciding factor in the Relationship, though Relationships Rated 13 do encourage beneficial things like personal growth for both partners. Low-Rated Relationships may work better for some; they also tend to be really interesting and show that both partners can be open to different Values. Partners with opposite Values also make versatile teams due to their diversity. These Relationships are not any less likely to last because of their low Rating - my grandparents have been married for 55 years and represent the union of a Skeptic with a Negotiator! The following list contains the Relationship Rating for each Cognietrics Relationship, with the highest number indicating the most favorable Relationship:

(Hopeful, Experimental) - 13

(Experimental, Hopeful) - 12

(Referential, Responsible) - 11

(Responsible, Referential) - 10

(Hopeful, Aggressive) - 9

(Referential, Rebellious) - 8

(Depressive, Experimental) - 7

(Avoidant, Responsible) - 6

(Aggressive, Hopeful) - 5

(Experimental, Depressive) - 5

(Rebellious, Referential) - 4

(Responsible, Avoidant) - 4

(Depressive, Aggressive) - 3

(Aggressive, Depressive) - 2

(Avoidant, Rebellious) - 1

(Rebellious, Avoidant) – 0

Game

You might enjoy a card game I invented some time ago called Cognietrics Poker.

There are 48 cards, 3 of each personality type. The deck is shuffled. Initial bets are placed. There are 2 cards dealt face-down to each person, and 1 card placed face-up in the center of the table. The total point value of each hand is determined by the relationship between the personality types on the cards in the hand, and the relationships of those personality types to the personality type on the card in the center of the table. Bets are placed again. Then, 1 card from each hand may be traded for 1 new card drawn from the deck. After, bets are placed one last time. The hands are shown. Whoever had the hand with the largest total point value wins. If multiple players have winning hands of equal total point value, then the pot is split between them.

*The Relationship Ratings for each Type can be found in the Type Profiles.

CHAPTER EIGHT

Nootypology

Until now this book has been a treatment of Cognietrics, a theory of mine that pertains to the implications of the four-letter Jungian codes for each Type. This chapter will address the Types with increased detail. Specifically, this chapter is about the psychological development to a more generalized mindset called the Nootype.

There is of course a philosophy of science to which Karl Popper made notable contributions, but is there a science of philosophy? Cognietrics uses Jungian psychological concepts to explain fundamental epistemological positions. However, while many philosophical points arise from Cognietrics, as it addresses Myers-Briggs typology it also shows the limitations. Though the four letters are behavioral expressions compatible with a certain combination of more complex philosophical Traits, the Triads themselves, from which the Preference definitions are in fact derivative, are Abelian subgroups and so have no purposeful direction, and even then ultimately just serve as philosophical evolutionary niches and groupings of convenience arranged to minimize complex operations and increase utility; however, the Nootypological Function Order has direction in time, and the Nootypological Functions themselves are also not niches, because they are binary opposites. At the end of Chapter 6 I mentioned some interesting points about the philosophical implications of the Triads to show that Cognietrics also has value and that Nootypology is more of an extension of Cognietrics, rather than a replacement. In fact, the Cognietric Types, once considered obsolete by the maturing mind (which now avoids Triad niche distractions by utilizing the traits of organization and leadership), become more useful as tools.

Short Nootypological Preferences Test

1. Are your accomplishments more a) competitive or b) creative?

2. Are your interests more a) practical or b) imaginative?

3. Are your decisions more a) emotional or b) logical?

4. Are you more a) flexible or b) rigid in your beliefs?

5. Are your projects a) focused individually or b) influenced with connections?

6. Are your solutions a) invented, b) discovered, or c) diversified?

7. Is your energy attained while a) alone, b) with friends, or c) in the service of a public cause?

Answer Key:

1. a) Achieving b) Generating

2. a) Sensing b) Dreaming

3. a) Feeling b) Thinking

4. a) Realizing b) Challenging

5. a) Maximizing b) Bridging

6. a) Perceiving b) Judging c) Organizing

7. a) Introvert b) Extravert c) Leader

Therefore someone who answered every question with the first option would be an Achieving Sensing Feeling Realizing Maximizing Perceiving Introvert, or an ASFRMPI.

As you can tell, the answer to #6 does not deal with the Reaction Demeanor because Nootype Functions are more complex. I have also dispensed with "N" for iNtuiting because I believe that with all of the extra letters it might be confusing. I have replaced it with "D" for Dreaming.

It would not be incorrect for a GDFCBJE who feels very strongly about C to write the letters in some other order such as CJEBFDG, and in fact I would encourage others to do this so that future analysis may be provided for what it means to have a letter towards the beginning or end. There are 7! Subtype orders for each of the 288 Nootypes, or 1,451,520 Subtypes total. I think that the general case, such as for example "O, J, or P towards the beginning", would also be fascinating. I, personally, am a TBGDIPR; in addition, having T first does not mean that I have a Thinking Function as my first Nootypological Function, or Catalyst; it means that I use T a lot regardless of which Functions I use or what purpose they serve. It is for this same reason that an INTP may have a higher N score than a T score while having Ti as a Referential Function, as is so with any Nootype and its Functions, and partially because self-awareness is a problem, such that Cognietrics and Nootypology remain largely philosophical studies rather than psychological ones, as they seek to explain the mind with fundamental logic rather than circumstantial evidence. I will use the standard order of letters for Nootypes in this book, however, to prevent confusion.

Leaders get energy from the public, and don't accommodate their self or others the way Introverts and Extraverts do.

Organizers do not necessarily judge or perceive as they work.

An example to illustrate the two Organizers is as follows: A Generator might be the first runner, perhaps seeing value where others do not, whereas an Achiever would be the fastest runner, and would want social status.

C and R determine the Main Function Order. B and M determine the Main Function Temperaments.

Bridging - combining different ideas.
BL - l e i
BE - e i l
BI - i l e
e→i - encouraging diversity.
i→l - volunteering contributions.
l→e - networking extensively.

Maximizing - amplifying unique potential.
MI - i e l
ME - e l i
ML - l i e
i→e - encouraging strengths.
e→l - monitoring continuously.
l→i - providing feedback.

Challenging - having rigid beliefs.
CJ - j p o
CP - p o j
CO - o j p
j→p - accumulating evidence.
p→o - encouraging regularity.
o→j - correcting problems.

Realizing - having flexible beliefs.
RO - o p j
RP - p j o
RJ - j o p
p→j - assessing conditions.
j→o - adjusting situationally.
o→p - noticing change.

A GDTRBPI has Main Functions Di Tl Ge.

In addition to the Cognietric Functions, there are 10 additional Nootype Functions for increased interactions.

Gi Designing
Ai Measuring
Ge Solving
Ae Inspiring

Fl Balancing
Tl Developing
Sl Coordinating
Dl Preparing
Gl Supporting
Al Advising

For Main Functions Az Cy Ex where A complements B, C complements D, and E complements F, the Order is:

Az Cy Ex Main
Fx Dy Bz Auxiliary
Cz Ey Ax Optimistic Desire
Bx Fy Dz Pessimistic Desire
Ez Ay Cx Optimistic Necessity
Dx By Fz Pessimistic Necessity

First Column - Catalyst (Past)
Second Column - Method (Present)
Third Column - Goal (Future)

Cognietric Types socialize with the Reaction Function. As babies are heavily reliant on adults and are not yet independent, it is the extraverted Function that is formed first. The Reaction Preference determines it because it is already fully formed by this time - decisive babies will promote success with either emotional or logical preconsiderations, and indecisive babies will heavily engage the tools of success once they imagine or find them. Occasionally they will have to assure others by taking personal responsibility for an alternative Contemplation Function that balances the initial decisive control (Je) or comprehensive study (Pe). If Contemplation afterwards is used as a position of Reference, this indicates introspection, so the tendency is towards being Introverted. If it continues secondarily as Responsibility, this indicates engagement, and thus Extraversion. This shows that the Values are more psychologically fundamental than the Manners when determining the Preferences, because the Id Functions are never once considered in the process of determining the Reaction. This arrangement is forgotten with age and replaced with Nootype Functions. The Nootype integrates leadership where it is most successful, either judgment, perception, or organization. Introverted and extraverted Functions are then similarly chosen and the three are arranged in a useful Order starting with the most meaningful. Cognietrics is therefore useful for small children as a means of learning and simultaneously imposing a degree of regularity on their intentions. They use a Cognietrics Type when young and a Nootype more as they mature by learning the value of organization and leadership.

There are 18 Nootypes for every Cognietric Type. A Cognietric Type with Functions Az By corresponds to the following Nootypes where O can equal A or G:

Ol Az By
Az Ol By
Az By Ol

Az Oy Bl
Az Bl Oy
Oy Az Bl

Al Oz By
Al By Oz
Oz Al By

*Oz By Al is not one, but is often used for anonymity.

Similar to the Cognietric Personas are the Nootypological Personas:

Realizing

D→T - Proof
D→F - Application
S→T - Adaptation
S→F - Priority

T→G - Tactic
T→A - Calculation
F→G - Wonder
F→A - Incentive

G→D - Insight
G→S - Option
A→D - Expansion
A→S - Review

Challenging

T→D - Thesis
T→S - Research
F→D - Standardization
F→S - Promotion

D→G - Conception
D→A - Foresight
S→G - Response
S→A - Engagement

G→T - Usefulness
G→F - Characterization
A→T - Improvement
A→F - Endorsement

There are also Nootypological Triads, though these represent social values.

Spiritualists (Givers)
MC - Believers
BR - Ambassadors

Materialists (Takers)
MR - Coaches
BC - Conquerors

Classicists (Conservative)
DT - Analysts
SF - Guardians

Progressives (Liberal)
DF - Idealists
ST - Inspectors

Operators (Skilled)
GF - Writers
AT - Technicians

Manufacturers (Influential)
GT - Architects
AF - Speakers

Activists (Liberating)
GD - Artists
AS - Warriors

Authorities (Controlling)
GS - Trainers
AD - Executives

Classicists are Governors, or Operating Authorities attempting to maintain the status quo, and Investors, or Manufacturing Activists pursuing the continuation of profitable projects. Progressives are Capitalists, or Manufacturing Authorities in competition, and Socialists, or Operating Activists looking for advancement.

Governors do not have Investor Ideal Matches and Capitalists do not have Socialist Ideal Matches, primarily because each wants to maintain or alter something in the opposite manner with respect to what the other party desires. These niches are useful in that the associated Nootypes would not otherwise get along, and so do not represent stagnation.

Ideal Match:

First Letter - opposite
Second Letter - opposite
Third Letter - opposite
Fourth Letter - same
Fifth Letter - opposite
Sixth Letter - same
Seventh Letter - L if L, I if E, E if I

The letter "L" does not change because leadership styles should not Complement each other; this would detract from either one as for the two Je or Fx Functions.

Generally, Nootypological Relationships improve as similar Functions to the Ideal Match move higher in the Order:

To calculate Compatibility Percentage:

For Ideal Match Functions:

A B C
D E F
G H I
J K L
M N O
P Q R

Set A = sqrt(18), B = sqrt(17), ... , Q = sqrt(2), R = sqrt(1).

To calculate the Compatibility Percentage for a Nootype with Functions:

N I C
J Q O...

Calculate (100/(18 + 17 + 16 + ... + 3 + 2 + 1))*(sqrt(5)*sqrt(18) + sqrt(10)*sqrt(17) + sqrt(16)*sqrt(16) ...).

Nootypological Functions correspond to Enneagram numbers. The order of influence of the Functions corresponds to the order of the numbers. I will explain it here, though like the Triads, it represents an evolutionary niche that gives only satisfactory control over a number of associated strategies.

The Main Function Order roughly corresponds to Enneagram Tritype.

Each number behaves as follows to balance the behaviors of the numbers immediately before and after it:

Balance of Forces

Je 1 Consultant - balancing mediation with campaigning.
Pe 2 Campaigner - balancing consultation with entrepreneurship.
Pl 3 Entrepreneur - balancing campaigning with individualism.
Pi 4 Individualist - balancing entrepreneurship with examination.
Oi 5 Examiner - balancing individualism with loyalty.
Oe 6 Loyalist - balancing examination with motivation.
Ol 7 Motivator - balancing loyalty with dare.
Jl 8 Darer - balancing motivation with mediation.
Ji 9 Mediator - balancing dare with consultation.

The Enneagram numbers represent strategies which the Nootype Functions assist. Wings represent an imbalance of tendencies that favors one force over the other. Introverted Functions correspond to withdrawn numbers, extraverted Functions correspond to compliant numbers, and leading Functions correspond to assertive numbers. Organizing Functions are located in the Head Center due to justifiability. Perceiving Functions are located in the Heart Center due to openness. Judging Functions are located in the Gut Center due to decisiveness. The middle of each Center suppresses it. Enneagram Tritypes choose a Head number, a Heart number, and a Gut number, with Wings, in any order. In Enneagram there are also Social (who look for approval),

Sexual (who look for chemistry), and Self-Preserving (who look for material comfort) Enneagram Subtype Instincts, but they have no anticipated correlation to Nootypology. Moving forward numerically on the diagram is Challenging due to the independent influence of the next balancing force, and within a Center it is Maximizing due to the completion of the Center's influence. The forward direction shows increases in computational complexity: Organizing forces move from Generation to Achievement; Perceiving forces move from Sensation to Dreaming; Judging forces move from Feeling to Thought. Likewise you know after understanding and you deduce after induction when learning about something relevant. The Bridging and Realizing directions allow receptivity to other ideas at a more basic level of familiarity.

    1w9 Fe
    1w2 Te
    2w1 Se
    2w3 De
    3w2 Sl
    3w4 Dl
    4w3 Si
    4w5 Di
    5w4 Gi
    5w6 Ai
    6w5 Ge
    6w7 Ae
    7w6 Gl
    7w8 Al
    8w7 Fl
    8w9 Tl
    9w8 Fi
    9w1 Ti

Notice that not all Enneagram Tritype strategies exist as a Nootype; for instance, 1w9-2w1-6w5 corresponds to

Fe Se Ge. While there are only 288 Nootypes, there are 1,296 Enneagram Tritypes, and for each Tritype there are six possible Instinctual Subtype Stackings. However, each correlation represents a niche and is not absolute, but can be useful. The strategies employed by the Enneagram Tritypes often require a fresh look and for that reason a Nootype will achieve more success with a Tritype that does not directly correlate to the Nootype Functions. For instance, I prefer to act as a 9w1-6w5-3w4 so/sx/sp, or Consulting Mediator, Examining Loyalist, and Individualist Entrepreneur, which while correlating to Aetiological, Solving, and Preparing strategies may be assisted instead by my Nootype's Statistical, Developing, and Solving Functions.

The complexity that is brought by increasing Enneagram numbers shows that:

Socialists Judge and Organize, or Perceive.
Capitalists Perceive and Organize, or Judge.
Investors Judge and Perceive, or Organize.
Governors Judge, Perceive, and Organize, or are completely open to new ideas.

***

Cognietrics, a formalization of concept definition that represents the selective pressures that competing psychological preferences have placed on philosophical concepts, measure the mutual interdependence of cognitive processes. The future of cognietrics can follow three paths. In anticognietrics, there would be a reason why someone intuitive and quick to decide would be considered reasonable. An example is that for Axiomatic pursuits Math is synthesized in a Visionary manner and Logic defined in a Scholarly way, whereas the opposite is true Contextually. In expanded cognietrics, additional traits beyond the original thirty would illuminate other aspects of the philosophical concepts in a web of similarly mutually interdependent definitions; I think that artificial intelligence is helpful (there is already a text classifier (https://www.uclassify.com/browse/g4mes543/myers-briggs-type-indicator-text-analyzer?input=Url) that identifies the author's type from a text sample), since factor analysis of the dictionary has yielded the Big 5, which correlate to the four Jungian preferences as found by A. Furnham in 1996 (https://doi.org/10.1016/0191-8869(96)00033-5) and a measure of mental health. Lastly, alternate cognietrics would illuminate unrelated verbal systems using the same architecture as cognietrics. There are also implications for language processing: In "this is specific to" you have axiom specific pattern. In "this happens when" you have axiom intuiting effect. You may sort this way to find effects, axioms, and prediction. If you have both types of axioms represented in a way relevant to each other you can make a connection between the two and find a new axiom. Triad Webs have high logical, conceptual, and ideational resolution. A Triad can imply many relations. In a related Triad what separate words entail the separate effects of the relations of the first Triad? As Conceptual Knowledge is Abstract uncertainty is implied. As Conceptual Abstraction is Knowledge possibility is implied. In Conceptual Literal Understanding uncertainty defines reliability and possibility defines anticipation. This type of word separation can act as a logical operator on relations and their effects on Triads. In this Triad Concept can only be defined by 'possibility' and 'uncertainty'. A related expression is "this is supposed to". Knowledge is Abstract when it's Conceptual because it is 'unproven'. Knowledge is Conceptual when it is Abstract because of the 'potential'. A related statement is "maybe". Abstraction is Knowledge when it is Conceptual because of 'relevance'. Abstraction is Conceptual when it is

Knowledge because of 'usefulness'. A related question is "why this?". These expressions can define the Triad: identify potential (this is supposed to) effects (why this?) using a model (maybe). I conjecture that if a law is described by these types of statements within the Triad then correlation with an event may more easily be dissected and anticipated. How are the minimum descriptive dimensions relevant to introverted achievement relations and the relation joining them to extroverted generation relations? How are the relations between all the resultant properties useful? Derivatives may be relations that are commutative with another relation (the derivative of Proof a way may be Tactic or Calculation) and may describe the partial derivative of that relation. What derivatives of a relation exist? Are they relevant to the actual derivatives? What can extroverted generation relations reveal about an independent variable internally to the dimension? Can multiple parametric equations show a common independent dimension internally such that the consistency of an internal logic is necessary some way and the applicability of the theory sufficient? Also what is the relevance of nonanalogous assumptions between the partial derivatives? You should now feel as though you have a solid understanding of each Type and its Relationships. Hopefully, what you have learned you will take with you so that it may serve you in your quest for knowledge and other related endeavors.

Happy Typing!

Alon Oscar Deutsch

Index

ABOUT THE AUTHOR

The theory of Cognietrics was created by Alon Oscar Deutsch, an INTJ. Reading from age 3 (a year after he had his first original Jungian ideas), he was a top point scorer (even winning arguments with judges) on his elementary school's book trivia team, which achieved a 1 of 23 ranking in the "Sunshine State Battle of the Books" trivia competition. A composer who began writing music at age 12 (including music for every Myers-Briggs type), he also performed with the varsity jazz band and was offered a record deal for his works. He first took an interest in Jung during a high school psychology class and began studying Myers-Briggs types towards the end of college, during which he took upper-level psychology electives such as Behavior Modification and Animal Behavior and philosophy electives such as Critical Thinking and Theory of Knowledge, all while conducting research laboratory experiments in molecular biophysics, neurochemistry, and optics, and later graduating with a degree in mathematics and physics. He was a National Merit Scholar and an Advanced Placement Scholar with Distinction in high school, a member of the Golden Key International Honour Society in college, and after scoring in the 99th percentile on the ASVAB he graduated top of his class from the United States Navy nuclear program, going on to serve aboard a nuclear submarine as a nuclear reactor operator. He is also a member of the International Society for Philosophical Enquiry, which represents the 99.9th percentile of IQ and standardized testing and is the oldest functioning genius-level intelligence network. A brain mapping by Dario Nardi shows preferred use of FP2, O1, F8, T4, F7, and F4, and past development of O1, T3, T4, T5, F8, and T6.

Appendix A

Function Questions

Ni/Se - what forces are acting?
Ne/Si - what can I do?
Pi - what affects me?
Pe - what can others teach me?
N - what may occur?
S - what is happening?
Ti/Fe - is this valuable?
Te/Fi - will this succeed?
Ji - am I achieving goals?
Je - can we do better?
T - does this make sense?
F - is this important?

*Introverts primarily use the introverted function and extraverts primarily use the extraverted function. Judgers introvert perception to minimize its effect on their behavior while still allowing them to check things thoroughly on the go. Perceivers introvert judgment to minimize its effect on their behavior while still allowing them to make the most of opportunities as they observe. Extraverts lead with the reaction function to build trust; introverts use the reaction function and its complement together only to overcome obstacles.

T to debate
F to distill
N to connect
S to detect

My girlfriend Michal Penn once described the origin of relativity as she thinks of it to me. Light in another reference frame is longer so mass energy equivalence means less Higgs interaction such that velocity is relativistic and the speed of light is constant in any reference frame; otherwise, charged particles can outrun the field and infinite acceleration over distance in a field brings infinite mass (so general relativity is accommodated in an unrelated spatial direction, the world line). The tendency to aggregate mass in one direction is counterbalanced by the tendency to aggregate mass differently in another direction. Relativity occurs during scattering momentum distribution and energy mass equivalence occurs during scattering collision. Cosmic expansion from mass can escape light.

A robot that only deals with the same things to do things is conceptual and might put things towards a new purpose to figure it out. If it can only deal with changes it deals with patterns and should apply them to an accepted purpose to keep the same context. An example is something anomalous in a typical process. Out of the typical instructions, what patterns tend to be relevant to each one? Statistical likelihood can order the results and other patterns can support artificial understanding.

I propose that when spacetime is warped Higgs bosons are removed allowing acceleration to the speed of light and motion in space such that large masses still have proportional momentum, and Higgs boson decay occurs in the opposite direction. When Higgs interactions become proportional to the impulse due to extra displacement the mass becomes proportionally more inertial and the velocity of the particle reflects the proportional increase in energy for the next collision or relativistic emission causing mass-energy equivalence.

Logic happens when necessity is consistency and theoretical application is sufficient. Questions about what isn't obvious, as told by Noam Chomsky in The Secrets of

Words, might be somewhat solved by the leftover Triads of a Triad group in a relevant way. Realizing Nootype relations can choose a word for a more common concept definition in axiom creation. Different words and their relations can be combined or resorted different ways though each axis has an inverse direction (change/op lessens consistency/po). Chaotic Concepts (Realizing) may be described by Patterns of Complexity (Challenging). Realizing cycle conceptually can't happen with logical necessity though logic can detract from it so it is only useful for falsification some way; science can also detract from logic. Logic is the response of the environment to words and the environment is made up of logical patterns. Complexity is the dependent variable whereas the independent variable must cumulatively reinforce in any physical formula because it will stop where the reinforcing elements fail. Complexity takes consistency, removes obstacles, and uses something relevant for positive feedback to again support the original consistency. Economics can be described with this type of mathematical relationship (such as supply and demand) in describing the cycle of knowledgeable decisions and what could strengthen a desired axis direction. For effective communication try using more of the extravert Functions such as Scouting when Sensing. Division of labor among robots can lessen the need for knowledge accumulation in AI. I believe that the decision making process could be resolved each time if an automated taxi could notice a consistency or change and choose the best action if all of the other conditions are right (from a library of possibilities). A text generator could similarly sort by statistical strength or input questions consistent data as it is relevant to useful actions and conditions as recombined from science journal searches. This taxonomy of knowledge addresses engineering and troubleshooting processes and may be useful to AI decision making such that priorities are noticed and accommodated:

P&O axis is empirical, high statistical correlations?

J&O axis is response, what should be done?

J&P axis is value, is it a good environment?

consistency adjustment observation

What is it doing?

consistency adjustment relevance

Why is it doing it?

consistency solution observation

How is it being handled?

consistency solution relevance

Why is it being solved?

change adjustment observation

What adjusted to the change?

change adjustment relevance

Why adjust to the change?

change solution observation

How did it handle the change?

change solution relevance

Why is it handling the change?

Quantized motion means that particles would push out on each other and not be synchronized culminating in multiple dimensions. Since the field can be planar and net force can do the same thing triangularly from both sides three dimensions must exist. The imbalance in acceleration away from one corner of the pyramid towards an area where no particles are collinear means that four dimensions aren't required, because the third particle forming the plane provides a degree of freedom.

The result of multiple AIs can be processed with image recognition and then by a taxonomy of knowledge then sorted by input questions or possible results. In error recognition an action that is not refuted by logical fallacies or other known problems and produces correct changes that produce correct and relevant conditions may guide the next correct action again without logical errors.

Complexity is the Pattern that the Concept did reinforce. The more the Concept contradicts its emergent Patterns the fewer imprints they leave in other dimensions the more a self-referential complexity is supported and it happens when the Concept is pervasive. Pattern is the response of the environment to the Concept. The only reason a Pattern exists is because other Patterns don't contradict it. Patterns and Concepts define each other and what can happen. If a critical point is breached mathematically in an imprinted dimension the Knowledge changes and if the Pattern changes the change can be Deduced and a different response can be chosen. If you change the Concepts you can Induct something.

Thinking AI can see if something changed and needs to be changed with regard to relevant logic. Reasoning AI can adapt to a recognized Pattern by upgrading parts for useful Concepts. The consistency from one AI may support relevance in another AI. Michal also showed that when integrating an AI from a consistency relevant aspects should be Perceived and Organizations should be characterized and addressed to solve a problem.

Causectivity (October 23rd, 2025)

1 All None
2 If Then
3 And Or
4 Specific General
5 Abstract Concrete
6 Progressive Stable
7 Input Output

123
If And None - This is the dependency.
Then Or None - This concerns uncertainty.
If Or All - This is the sufficient condition.
Then And All - This is the necessary condition.

156
All Abstract Stable - This concerns axioms.
All Concrete Progressive - This provides balance.
None Abstract Progressive - This concerns probability.
None Concrete Stable - This concerns time.

147
All Specific Input - This allows an understanding of events.
All General Output - These are the effects.
None Specific Output - These are the confound effects.
None General Input - These are the confound causes.

245
If Specific Concrete - These are the logical antecedents.
If General Abstract - This concerns possibilities.
Then Specific Abstract - These are the exact conceptual causes.
Then General Concrete - These are the resultant tendencies.

267

If Progressive Input - This is how axioms cause changes.

Then Stable Input - This concerns reliability.

If Stable Output - Similar antecedents should have similar effects.

Then Progressive Output - This is the form that the changes have.

346

And Specific Stable - This is the entire formula.

Or General Stable - This shows what is excluded.

And General Progressive - This concerns typical reactivities.

Or Specific Progressive - This shows analogy.

357

And Concrete Output - This concerns the multiplicity of resultant effects.

And Abstract Input - This is Quine Duhem Thesis, that no theory is tested in isolation.

Or Concrete Input - This concerns relevance.

Or Abstract Output - This isolates causal chains.

*If Concrete relations imply Abstract relations and something is falsified that part is inductively invalid.

**The consistency, relevance, and usefulness of If in a logical assertion may be of concern to the patterns it affects.

***If two fields are described in the triad web does the definition of an interstitial triad that combines traits from both fields help the opposing fields?

The Reason for Jungian Typology: Heraclitus said, "if there is one thing that is immutable, it is change". Naturally our responses to such an unpredictable idea differ as they evolve to meet it. We may ask: Should I be concerned with specific (Introverted) or general (Extraverted) change? This is important because the very concept of change implies degrees of change. Should I respond to change (Sensing) or initiate it (iNtuiting)? This is important because we are both agents and experiencers of change. Should I work to change things based on things that aren't changing (Thinking) or slow things that are (Feeling)? This is important because change can be positive or negative. Should I act before (Judger) or after (Perceiver) change? This is important because changes may bring about other changes. I believe the exploration of the degrees of change (IE) reflects changes in things that have not functionally changed from each other, whereas the exploration of the results of change (JP) reflects changes in things that have functionally changed from each other. This distinction in categorization is what allows us to define both the observational differences that prevent vagueness and the utilitarian implications that prevent triviality, both of which comprise change, so both are quite important. I believe the ability to experience and respond to change (SN) reflects the recognition of change, that implies change in the universe and which alone would seem hopeless, and the ability to slow or hasten change (TF) reflects the ability for deliberateness, that implies lack of change in the universe and which alone would seem meaningless. The combination makes change important to our species. These ideas, the defining and motivating aspects of change handled by the preferences that are the minimum needed to organize one's mind, show that it is real and important, and collectively manifest in the immutable aspects of our existence. For this reason I think that the four Myers-Briggs dichotomies are both necessary and sufficient for categorizing psychological preference.

THE END